CRYING WIND

The masterful

storyteller

weaves stories

of laughter

and love, pain

and triumph

When the Stars Danced

Sequoyah
EDITIONS

WHEN THE STARS DANCED
by Crying Wind

A Sequoyah Edition
An imprint of Indian Life Books
A Division of Intertribal Christian Communications

ISBN 0-920379-19-2

First published November 2001

Cover and interior design by Uttley/Douponce DesignWorks,
Sisters, Oregon   www.uddesignworks.com

Inside cover text written by Nan McKenzie Kosowan

Unless otherwise marked, all Scripture quotations are from
the Holy Bible, King James Version

Printed and bound in Canada

Visit Indian Life Ministries' website at www.indianlife.org
and Crying Wind's website at www.cryingwind.com

DEDICATION

This book is dedicated to all the wonderful people who read *Crying Wind* and *My Searching Heart*, and who wrote asking me to write another book about my family.

This book was not easy to write. It is easy to share our best times with you, it is easy to share our laughter with you, it is far more difficult to share our worst times and our failures and our tears.

If I've learned one thing in life, it is that every day is filled with surprises and that life doesn't have to be perfect to be good.

Thank you for being part of our family.

A special thank you to my forever-friends, Joanie H. and Denise W. You have always been there for me.

I also want to thank my children, Little Antelope, Lost Deer, Snow Cloud and Spring Storm, for your courage, your loyalty and your love. When you were born, the stars danced in the sky!

—CRYING WIND

Crying Wind, author of the best selling books, *Crying Wind* and *My Searching Heart,* grew up on the Kickapoo and Navajo reservations. She received the Kiowa Indian name, "Mahnsaw Dayna", meaning "Hummingbird", in recognition for her distinguished Christian service and in the tradition of the highest honor of the American Indian and Eskimo people.

Crying Wind currently lives between two volcanoes on the Big Island of Hawaii where she continues to write novels and paint pictures to record and preserve native legends and lifestyles.

FOREWORD

I have two treasured gifts. Two books by Crying Wind. I have both—*Crying Wind* and *My Searching Heart*—on my shelf. These were gifts from my mother-in-law who was an evangelist and a quarter blood Choctaw. She died two years ago, but would be delighted to know a third book is in the wind by this wonderful author.

Once again, the masterful storyteller, Crying Wind, weaves stories of laughter and love, family and faith. From a story circled with colorful marbles to the triumph of daughters-in-law in the laundry war; from unexpected loss to Providential gain, Crying Wind shares her own family journey. Through her honesty and simplicity, we dance along with the stars celebrating God's faithfulness and provision, and His everlasting love.

I congratulate Crying Wind and Indian Life Books on the publication of this fine, inspiring story.

—JANE KIRKPATRICK
Award-winning author of *Love to Water My Soul*
and *Mystic Sweet Commmunion*

PREFACE

When I wrote my first book, *Crying Wind,* I poured out my heart. I believed God had given me a story to tell and wanted me to share it with people who were lost and lonely and needed hope and encouragement. The thousands of wonderful letters I received from people proved the message in the book was reaching out and touching lives.

I'd worked closely with the editor and staff of a publisher and we discussed changes in my book. Shortly after the book was published, the publishing company changed management and new editors and policies were brought in. All the editors and staff I'd worked with either resigned or were let go. I was working with strangers who didn't know me or my books and problems developed.

I made mistakes. I tried too hard to please the wrong people. The publisher felt my books were too controversial and stopped publishing them.

I felt hurt and betrayed and never wanted to write again . . . but God had other plans and said, "You aren't finished yet."

A month later, Harvest House Publishers agreed to publish my books. The editors and staff were committed to the highest Christian ideals and we worked together happily and successfully for many years.

God once again spoke to my heart and said, "Your story is not finished. . . ."

My special thanks to Jim Uttley and the staff at Indian Life Books for reaching out to me and making it possible to share my story and continue my ministry. I have been greatly blessed by many kind and good people who have walked through my life, who have loved me, helped and encouraged me and I carry them in my heart.

—CRYING WIND

Table of Contents

Chapter One

In the Heart of a Child

*I'd rather write my name in the heart
of a child than any other place in the world.*

L ife is full of strange and wonderful surprises. After my first two books were published they were translated into fifteen languages and published around the world. It was very exciting to my children to know that other children in China, Japan and the farthest corners of the world were reading about our family and sharing our lives.

I was invited to speak at churches, conventions and to appear on television programs.

I don't like to be away from my family and I especially don't like to fly on airplanes. I know God can take care of me when I'm on the ground, but I have trouble believing He can take care of me when I'm sitting in a metal tube, miles above the earth, hurtling through space at hundreds of miles an hour.

In spite of this fear, I felt God had given me a rare opportunity to share my faith and tell the story of our people. It was

11

time to give something back to God and to all the people who had made a difference in my life.

My husband, Don, was able to arrange his work schedule so he could stay home with our children during the four or five days a month I was gone. I turned down most of the speaking engagements and book tours I was offered because I couldn't bear being away from my family. It was always difficult to choose which ones to accept.

The publisher's secretary, Sharon, called me about the latest tour they planned for me. "I have you scheduled for an important television interview on January twelfth." Sharon was almost squealing with delight. "It's in Chicago and you'll be on the most popular talk show in the nation, millions of people will be watching! We'll not only sell thousands of books but this is only the beginning; we've already scheduled you to do twenty television interviews from California to New York!"

"I can't go anyplace on the twelfth," I said. "It's Snow Cloud's sixth birthday: I have to be home for my son's birthday."

"You can't be serious! You can't pass up this interview for a child's birthday party. Tell your son you'll celebrate a couple of days early. He's only six, he won't know the difference," Sharon said.

"A month from now no one will remember who was on television that day, but I'll never forget missing my son's birthday and neither will he," I explained. "Please try to schedule the interview for another date and tell them I have to bake a birthday cake shaped like a car that day."

Sharon was very unhappy when she hung up. She was even more unhappy when she called back an hour later. "I called the television producer. He said they couldn't schedule their show around birthday parties and they will just replace you with another guest," she said in a tone of voice that was supposed to make me feel guilty. "You missed a very important opportunity and it could hurt your career."

"My family is my career," I said.

That was several years ago. Every time Snow Cloud's birthday arrives he smiles and asks, "Remember my sixth birthday when you turned down that big television show just to be at home with me?"

"You are worth it. I wouldn't miss your birthday to be with five kings and a president," I tell him.

"I know," he answers.

Although I appreciated all the good things my publisher had done for me and his work promoting my books, we could not resolve our conflict about my traveling. He wanted me to be away from home three weeks of each month for personal appearances. I had originally agreed to be away from home four or five days a month and even that had become too painful. My children were too young to travel with me. I had to make a choice.

I knew there would be those who felt I had let them down, that God had given me work to do and a story to tell and that I was not doing the work I'd been called to do. I also knew that if I refused to go on the tours to promote the books that I would be fired, my books would go out of print and it would be a financial disaster to our family who had just bought a beautiful ranch in the mountains.

I knew the cost was going to be great. But I knew the cost of being away from my family was even greater.

My publisher canceled my contract. My books were taken off the market. We put our home up for sale.

People often asked how I could give up the crowds and the attention and the television interviews to stay at home.

"It's easy," I would answer, "I'd rather be famous at home and unknown to the rest of the world than to be famous everywhere in the world and be a stranger at home."

Less than a month later a new publisher contacted me about putting my books back into print: he said I would not have to travel unless I wanted to.

God had heard my prayers and made it possible for me to have the best of both worlds. My message would be heard but I could stay at home with my family. Of course, there were still a few surprises waiting for us.

My husband is usually a very calm, quiet man but sometimes even he can get pushed to the breaking point.

"Crying Wind, who was that?" Don gasped when a man wearing nothing but a robe walked through our kitchen and headed for the bathroom.

"I don't know," I said as I poured myself a cup of coffee, "but the rest of his family is setting up their camper in our front yard."

"But WHO are they?" Don's voice had become rather loud.

"Well, when I spoke to that Christian Bookseller's Convention in Chicago last winter, I ended my speech by saying that if any of them were ever in Colorado to stop by for coffee. I think someone has come for their cup of coffee," I explained.

"But there were six thousand people at that convention. Who are these people in our yard?" Don asked.

"The lady outside said I would remember her because she wore a blue dress and waved at me," I answered.

"It's going to be a long summer," Don said as he swallowed two aspirin.

We lived fifty miles from the nearest town but that summer more than one hundred and fifty people "dropped in for coffee". They took flowers from our garden, took endless photographs of our family, asked me to make moccasins for them and one family asked if we would let their grandmother live with us because they really couldn't stand her anymore. People borrowed tools, bedding and money and a lady from Iowa asked me to wash up a few things for them because little Jimmy had been carsick. I fed them lunch while I washed their laundry.

People arrived at any time during the day or night and more than once arrived after we'd gone to bed. It's not easy for Don to be friendly after midnight.

A man escaped from a mental hospital in Maine after reading my book, *Crying Wind*. He believed voices told him we were meant to be man and wife and he hitchhiked all the way to Colorado to marry me. He arrived on my porch and when I explained to him I was already married and had children he went into a rage and I had to call the sheriff and have him taken away.

The man had spent twenty years in the mental institution and because his doctors considered him violent and dangerous and because he'd escaped, he was placed in an institution with tighter security. He'd been a serious threat not only to us, but to everyone who'd given him a ride or come into contact with him while he traveled across the country. Other than frightening us, he hadn't harmed us. We became very nervous about visitors after that.

One newspaper interview mentioned that our family always attended a certain church every Sunday. When we returned home from church on one occasion, we found the house had been burglarized, the thief had even stolen the food out of the freezer. It bothered me that my home could no longer be the warm and welcoming place I'd dreamed about.

Don and I agreed we had to regain our privacy and never,

under any circumstances, was I to invite six thousand people to drop in for coffee, no matter how nice they were.

The mail was always wonderful. Many people wrote to me after reading my books; hundreds of letters came from children all around the world. I became a pen pal with many people, making friendships that lasted for years. I like letters because they don't wake me up at night, they don't ask me to do laundry and they don't get me into trouble. Well, most of the time they don't get me into trouble.

I received a frantic letter from Dorothy, a woman in her sixties, who told me she was a good, honest woman who never did anything crazy. However, when her ladies' book club reviewed my book, that snooty old Rachael Thurston bragged that she was going to write to Crying Wind and ask for her autograph. For some reason, something just snapped inside Dorothy and she said she was one of my closest friends.

Dorothy, who was always so quiet and shy, was suddenly the center of attention and she loved the look of envy on Rachael's face. Dorothy threw caution to the wind and went a step further to announce she was having lunch with me on Friday. Her moment of glory backfired when everyone in the ladies' book club asked to come along to have lunch with us.

Her letter begged me to meet her at the restaurant on Friday and pretend we were old friends. She said she'd wear a pale pink dress with a string of pearls so I could recognize her. She'd understand if I didn't come because I must think she was insane and if I didn't show up, she'd admit to her club that she'd lied and she'd resign because that awful old Rachael would make her life miserable. She was terribly sorry for the whole mess.

I folded up her letter. There was only one thing to do.

Friday, I arrived at the restaurant, threw my arms around Dorothy's neck and raved on and on about how dear she was to me. We had a delightful luncheon, Dorothy was so grateful she didn't know whether to laugh or cry. Rachael was a very cold and unlikeable woman and I could understand why Dorothy had acted the way she had.

I guess we've all had a Rachael Thursten in our lives at one time or another. We all ate delicious turkey sandwiches except for Rachael who ate crow.

The best thing about that day was Dorothy and I became real friends and met often for lunch and a good visit. She always said that when I walked into the restaurant she felt like a troop of Mounties had arrived to rescue her.

Thanks, Dorothy, it isn't very often that I get to feel like a real hero.

It's strange how, just when you think you have your life all planned, something or someone will turn it upside down.

"Let's move," Don said.

I spent the next few weeks crying, pouting, sulking and whining. I loved our home. I'd expected to spend the rest of my life here, not just a brief four years. I knew he was right. We were too isolated and as they grew older, it was going to be hard for the children to live so far away from other people. The winters in the mountains were long—we were often snowed in for a week at a time—and the summers were short. I'd never liked the bitter cold weather of the high mountains.

Don wanted to move to a warmer place, closer to civilization, someplace where we could have privacy and live a normal life again.

Don, who is sensible and cautious, opened a map of the United States and spread it out on the kitchen table. He closed his eyes and put his finger down. He opened his eyes and said, "I guess we are moving to Cow Skin, Missouri."

I've never fainted in my life but I came closer at that moment than at any other time.

Our beautiful mountain home was sold and was going to be turned into a church retreat. It was renamed "Praise Mountain", and as much as it hurt to say goodbye to our ranch we had called

"Thundering Hills," I was grateful for all the spiritual awakenings and soul mending that would take place here for weary Christians. I felt God had allowed our home to be chosen for this special purpose to make it easier for us to let it go.

Another two weeks of crying (me, not the children), found us settled on a farm located half way between Cow Skin and Possum Flats, Missouri. In other words, Don had dragged us all to the end of the world. One farmer told us we were so far in the hills that even God had to have two road maps and a compass to find us. We were doomed.

Chapter Two

I REMEMBER LOVING YOU...

Don and I have been married twenty-six years. We have still not found one thing we have in common.

In the Spring, he plants vegetables to feed the body. I plant flowers to feed the soul.

I'm always cold and turn up the heat. He's always hot and opening windows.

I love the sound of Indian drums and chants at pow-wows and opera. Don loves country music and the sound of guitars and banjos and songs about old dogs and trucks.

I like anything chocolate. He likes steak and potatoes.

In twenty-six years we've never agreed on anything. The funny thing is, we don't disagree either. Our marriage isn't perfect, in fact, there have been times I considered shooting arrows at him!

We've just accepted the fact that we are such complete opposites it is hopeless to try to change each other. I tell people we don't argue because we are mature, sensible people devoted to our family and dedicated to God. Don tells people we don't argue because raising four children leaves you too exhausted to disagree about anything.

Our farm is one inch deep. That means there is about one inch of dirt before you hit solid rock. It is hard to grow a garden on a rock, but Don tries every year.

On March 17th, Saint Patrick's Day, he plants potatoes. Other vegetables are planted by the phases of the moon but potatoes are always planted on Saint Patrick's Day.

Don hoes and waters and weeds, he fights the weather and the rabbits and deer that sneak into the garden and eat the tender plants. He waits to harvest his crop with the same excitement as a child waiting for Christmas. He has never really wanted to do anything but be a farmer, nothing would make him happier than having his sons grow up and work the farm with him. He dreams of having a big farm someday and giving a few acres to each of the children when they marry so they will have a good home for their families.

"Look, Cry!" he proudly points to the new potatoes, "I dug up a whole bushel."

"How many did you plant?" I asked.

"Four bushels, I did better this year than I did last year," he brags, "I figured it up and I think it comes to about seventy-five dollars."

"You mean we only went seventy-five dollars in the hole this year on your garden?" I asked.

"Yep, last year I lost about a hundred dollars on my garden. I think at this rate, in a few more years we'll break even," he says hopefully. "I think I'll go look at some seed catalogs, it's not too early to start thinking about next year's garden. If we don't get too much sun, or too much rain and if the deer don't get the early crop and if I spend about a hundred hours hoeing weeds, we might only lose about fifty dollars on the garden next year."

One of the things I like about Don is that he is such an optimist. He has never wasted a penny in his life but he has thrown away thousands of them.

"A penny saved is a penny wasted," he says, "But find a penny and pick it up and all day long you'll have good luck. Do you know what the poorest boy in town has in common with the richest man in town?" he asked Little Antelope. "They'll both bend over to pick up a lucky penny and they'll both smile. The only thing you can buy with a penny is a smile."

Just to make sure there are enough lucky pennies to go around, Don throws away about a hundred pennies every week. He scatters them on school playgrounds and parks and sidewalks.

"How many pennies do you think you've planted?" I asked.

"Oh, I guess about fifty thousand or more. Just think, if only half of them were found, I've made twenty-five thousand people smile and feel lucky for a minute. That's not such a small thing," he answered.

"It's a real bargain," I agreed.

Lost Deer and Snow Cloud are at the age where they want to have big muscles and they try to lift everything on the farm from rocks to young calves.

"How much weight can you lift, Dad?" Snow Cloud asked.

"Well, son, I can lift two hundred and fifty pounds but I can't carry it very far," he answered.

He doesn't mention that sometimes he carries the weight of the world on his shoulders. Don is physically and morally strong but he never boasts or brags. He just takes it for granted that a man does what's right and takes care of his family and helps others when he can.

Don is the strongest man I've ever known. He can cook and sew and iron and bake cookies. He can lift two hundred-pound sacks of oats to feed the cows as easily as he can sew a button on his daughter's coat. To him, there is no difference between "man's work" and "woman's work," all work has the same value and all of it is necessary for the survival of the family.

The sidewalk in front of the house is badly cracked. Don and I spend a lot of time talking about repairing it before someone trips and falls but it is one of those jobs you can put off almost forever.

Don bought the cement and the boards to build the frame and we decided the first thing tomorrow morning we'd repair the sidewalk. We sat in the yard and discussed our new sidewalk and how much better it would look, and of course, how much safer it would be.

While we sat on the porch steps, the children crawled along the sidewalk playing with their toy cars.

The cracks made perfect roads for their cars to travel.

"Tomorrow, I'm making a new sidewalk," Don told the kids.

Lost Deer looked up.

"Will it be just like this one?" he asked.

"Better," Don said, "It will be wider and there won't be any cracks."

All four children stopped playing and stared at us.

"A sidewalk has to have cracks," Lost Deer said, "we need cracks for our roads."

"Daddy, the butterflies use the cracks for road maps, they won't know how to find flowers if they can't see their road maps when they fly over our yard," Snow Cloud said.

"Daddy," Spring Storm's eyes filled with tears,
"these are fairy roads, they are the only roads fairies have to get home at night. They'll get lost!"

"Now what?" I whispered to him.

Don looked at me and then at the children.

"I didn't know those cracks were so important. I guess we'd better save them so the fairies and butterflies won't get lost," he said.

The children went back to their play, pushing their little cars around.

"We'll fix the sidewalk someday when they are older," he shrugged.

At that moment, I loved him too much to speak.

LOVING YOU

I remember,
The way the stars danced in the sky,
And lilacs bloomed,
And perfumed,
Misty meadows,
And I remember loving you.
I remember,
Hot summer nights,
Butterfly maps,
Fairy roads,
And I remember loving you.
I remember,
Carpets of frost,
Silver moss,
Christmas snow,
And I remember loving you.
I remember loving you,
I still do.

Chapter Three

GOODBYE, SPIRIT HORSE

I 've spent my life on the road less traveled. I miss the days when I was a child, running wild on the reservation, running wild in leather moccasins, listening to the fringe on my buckskin jacket slap against itself in the wind.

When I was young, I believed in Spirit Horses. They carried you away when the moon was silver and the wind was wild. You could ride across the sky and gallop through the clouds and dance with the stars. There is something powerful and magical about horses: they are one of God's most beautiful creations. I miss galloping my horse into the moonlight and feeling the night wind against my face. I miss being young and free.

I have a restless heart. I still want to wander in the mountains and across the desert and I want my children to have hearts that are free to fly and wander and run. I am always ready to wander. I never spend more time on my house than I spend on my family. A house is where I live. My family is why I live. If I'm washing dishes and one of the children says, "There is a jonquil almost ready to bloom in the yard…" I stop what I'm doing and go to the yard to look at the flower. I can't count the times I've been in the middle of cooking dinner and one of the children will holler, "Come and look at the sunset, it's like red gold!" I'll turn off the stove and join them in the yard. A sunset lasts minutes, a memory lasts a lifetime. Dinner can wait.

When a child asks you to spend time with them, it isn't an interruption, it's an invitation.

My children have led me through fairy-like tunnels of frosted limbs in the forest. They've shown me flocks of wild geese flying against a full moon. We've picked armloads of wild flowers, run with red foxes, touched a mountain lion, discovered dinosaur bones and explored caves. How could I ever give up the best times of my life to mop the floor or dust the furniture? Housework can wait until…Jonquils stop blooming in the yard and wild geese stop flying overhead. Housework can wait until no one says, "Quick, Mom, you have to come and see this!"

I've always loved the lines from the poem by Robert Frost,

> *The woods are lovely, dark and deep,*
> *But I have promises to keep,*
> *And miles to go before I sleep,*
> *And miles to go before I sleep.*

I think that somehow I'd have stolen a few minutes to wander those woods before I went home.

When I had a baby people warned me, "Just wait until he reaches the terrible twos." Well, one by one, the children reached their "twos" and they weren't terrible at all. A two-year-old is darling. They can walk and talk and reason and they are terrific.

When my children grew older, people said, "Just wait until they are teenagers." I have four teenagers. They can walk, talk and reason and they are terrific.

I've enjoyed my children at each age and phase they've gone through. I've never been disappointed in any of them, not that they are perfect, but sometimes it's our flaws that make us the most lovable.

I never spanked my children. I never believed hitting a person made them smarter or kinder or better. I always believed hitting a person only hurt them and made me less of a human being.

Luckily, God blessed me with the world's worst singing voice. I sound like a cat caught in a fight with a coyote. I have such a bad singing voice that it can only be used as a weapon. If the kids fought…I would start singing and it wouldn't take long before they forgot why they were fighting and would cover their ears and run for cover. Now they are teenagers and I don't have to sing anymore—I only have to threaten them. "If you aren't home before midnight, I'll sing in front of your friends . . ." They are never late.

$$* \ * \ *$$

My children believe I'm overprotective. Considering some of the near disasters we've survived, I don't think I'm protective enough.

We had an orphaned calf that weighed only a few pounds. Its coat was like black velvet and its huge brown eyes pleaded for love. I wrapped it in a towel and held it in my arms and fed it milk from a bottle. We named him Baby and we gave him gallons of milk and loved him and he lived and grew. And grew. Baby became a frisky little calf who played in the yard with the dogs and would run to me when I went outside with his bottle. Baby grew bigger but he never forgot the days when I held him and fed him with a bottle and whenever he saw me he'd come running. It was funny and cute until Baby became a thousand-pound bull who still wanted to be cuddled and petted. Being chased across the pasture by a half-ton bull, who is expecting a bottle of milk, stops being cute and becomes frightening. Baby didn't know a playful butt with his head could crush our bones.

It became ridiculous when we would stop at the gate to see where Baby was grazing and then make a mad dash to the barn to put out the feed before Baby saw us. Baby loved our family to death. It was my fault, I'd spoiled him and now he was dangerous. We'd have to sell Baby before he squashed one of us.

The last morning we had him, I went to the pasture with a bottle of milk. "Baby!" I called.

He came running, his eyes wide, his nostrils flared and his hooves pounding the ground. He stopped inches away and began drinking from the bottle. I patted his soft black coat. "I'll miss you, Baby," I said and I meant it. It was my fault we had to sell him and I felt badly about it. I hadn't let him grow up. Now he was going to some other farm where he'd be with a herd and produce wonderful calves, he'd eat grass and be called "Tornado" or "Lightning" or something more suitable for a bull. No one would call him "Baby" and feed him from a bottle. He had to grow up. I had to let go.

"You'll have to let us grow up someday," Little Antelope said, "When are you going to cut the apron strings?"

On his sixteenth birthday Little Antelope received some nice gifts but was puzzled when he opened a box from me and it held a long pink ribbon.

"What is this?" he asked, holding it up with two fingers.

"You asked me to cut the apron strings, so I did," I said.

He looked in the box again.

"There is only one apron string in here," he said. "When are you going to cut the other one?"

"Never," I smiled.

I thought growing pains were something that happened to children. I was wrong. They are something that takes place in a mother's heart. They feel like rocks grinding together under the weight of a slow moving glacier.

One of the nicest compliments I ever had came from a stranger.

"You are the kind of mother," she said, "who keeps the cookie jar filled and leaves it down where the kids can reach it." I never forgot her words and the cookie jar has become a special symbol of my love for my children.

Some mothers don't allow their children to have cookies because they feel other choices are healthier. I respect their decision. Parents must decide what is best for their own children. Personally, I believe there is a lot of comfort in a chocolate chip cookie.

Chapter Four

SO DEAR TO OUR HEARTS

It followed me home, Mom, can I keep it?" If you live in the city, this usually means your child has brought home a stray kitten or a puppy. If you live in the country it could mean anything from a chicken to a pig. Today it was a goat.

"Isn't she beautiful, Mom?" Snow Cloud hugged the smelly black nanny goat that looked at me with blank eyes that showed no signs of intelligence.

"She looks very valuable. I'm sure some farmer has lost her and wants her back." I hoped that was true.

"I'll put an ad in the lost and found and if nobody claims her in a week, can I keep her?" he begged.

"Okay," I agreed, not realizing I had just destroyed my entire life.

No one claimed the goat even though I ran the ad in the paper an extra week. Some very smart farmer had dumped his goat on our doorstep and wasn't about to plead guilty.

Nanny Goat ate every living thing in the yard except the cat.

She mowed the flowers to the ground and danced on the hood of the car. She grew and grew until it became obvious that she was great with child. Just before Christmas she produced triplets. That night an ice storm came sweeping through and the goats had to be moved into the house to keep them from freezing to death. That was also the night our minister came to visit. He said he'd never known anyone who kept goats in their living room before. He only stayed a few minutes. He said he wanted to get home before the roads got too slick. Nanny chewing on his shoelaces probably didn't help.

We discovered a goat only four hours old can jump onto a chair, bounce on a sofa and slide across the coffee table forty-two times an hour. Triplets can do one hundred twenty-six jumps, bounces and slides per hour. Nanny sat in the recliner, chewed her cud and showed no signs of intelligence.

The Christmas Parade in the village was just around the corner and what animal reminds us all of Christmas more than a goat and three baby goats? Don promised to take the goats to the parade in his truck but he was late getting home and we would miss the parade unless I drove my four children and the four goats in the car six miles to town. I'd have to be crazy to do that.

Nanny loved riding in the car but she insisted on a window seat. She sat upright with a seat belt holding her securely in place. Three of the children each held a baby goat. As other cars passed us people stared and pointed and I hoped they knew I had four goats in my car and not four very ugly children.

When we arrived in town, Snow Cloud dressed the four goats in tinsel, bobbles and bells and followed the band and the float with Santa Claus down the street.

The band struck up "Hark, the Herald Angels Sing", the goats bolted through the middle of the trumpet players and made short work of the elves. Santa jumped off the float and helped us corner the goats in the doorway of the Donut Shop. The goats were dragged back out onto the street and placed at the front of the parade to keep them as far away from the band as possible.

Snow Cloud and his goats won Second Place trophy for the most unusual entry. Nanny's picture was in the newspaper and she looked beautiful and brilliant. I was in the background of the photo, showing no sign of intelligence.

I remember seeing pictures of Jesus holding little lambs tenderly in his arms. Jesus, the Good Shepherd. It seemed like an easy life, just walking through meadows and sitting on grassy hills, watching the sheep and goats graze. Sometimes he would lead them beside still waters for a drink. Being a shepherd was a terrific occupation. That's what I thought until we had sheep and goats of our own.

I discovered they need constant care. They are silly, get sick easily and do incredibly stupid things. We've pulled sheep out of the pond and goats out of trees. They don't have enough sense to come in out of the rain (or anything else) and they can't get too hot or too cold or they die. If a sheep gets too frightened he might just lay down and die from sheer terror. Goats will try to jump anything, even if they kill themselves in the attempt. They have to be put into barns or corrals at night so coyotes or dogs don't kill them. I can go out to the barn thirty mornings in a row and lead them to the pasture and they'll follow in a nice, orderly line. Then one morning, for no particular reason, they'll mistake me for a wolf and run in fifty different directions, managing to destroy everything in their path, especially if it was anything I cared about.

The sheep's odd behavior seems familiar to me. I can't count the times I've followed God so closely I must have walked in his shadow and then, for no particular reason, I'd bolt like sheep and run in the opposite direction as fast as I could go. I know better, just like our sheep know better, but that doesn't stop either of us from being rebellious and foolish. At other times, I'll get so discouraged, I'll feel like lying down and dying from sheer panic, just like a sheep.

I know for the rest of my life I'll walk in the Good Shepherd's shadow most of the time but there will be other times I'll leap the fence and bounce off across the hills looking for my own greener pastures.

Like the other sheep, I'm not bad, I'm just sometimes stubborn and sooner or later, all of us lost sheep get tired and hungry and afraid and remember who our shepherd really is and we run home again.

The Lord is my shepherd.

It was an accident that ended with a goat farm and over the next few years, hundreds of goats came and went. We loved them all and as often as not, I cried when we sold them. I discovered each goat has a unique personality and they each left a memory.

"Do you remember Nanny and Prissy and Pigamia?" someone will ask and we'll all laugh because they were so awful and so smelly and so dear to our hearts. Days and seasons were marked and remembered by the animals that came and went through our lives. We saved some animals and lost others, we chased some and were chased by others. Each one left a memory, a smile, a tear, but each one made our lives a little richer.

Don has a habit of bringing home surprises. He might bring home an unusual rock he found while he was repairing the fence in the west pasture or he might bring home a beautiful turquoise ring that he bought at the trading post. Today he brought home two horses in the back of his truck.

"They are beautiful!" I said as he unloaded them into the corral. "But when you left the house, you said you were going to the store to buy some bread and cheese."

"I forgot the bread and cheese," he said as he watched the sleek red roan prance around, followed by the smaller, cream-colored horse. "On the way to the store I saw a friend of mine with these two horses and he said he was taking them to the sale. I told him I might buy them for the kids if he didn't want too much." He grinned.

"How much were they?" I asked, not that I cared. I was in love with them already.

"My friend said I could have the horses for free under one condition," he glowed with pride.

"What is the condition?" I asked.

"That we keep both horses until they die," Don said.

"That's a good deal, who could ever sell these wonderful horses?" I was excited and grateful for our good fortune.

"The red horse is called Star and the white one is called Coco," he pointed at them.

Star walked through the door into the barn. Coco walked into the side of the barn, bumped his head, turned around in circles and whinnied.

"He didn't see the barn," Don said and walked up and looked into Coco's eyes. "He's blind," he sighed, "He is completely blind. No wonder my friend was so generous."

"Oh, the poor thing! We'll have to take care of him so he won't hurt himself," I said, wondering how we'd take care of a blind horse. Star came out of the barn and nickered at Coco who hurried over to him and followed him to the water trough. They both took a long drink, then Star returned to the barn and Coco followed inches behind him.

"A horse leading a blind horse?" I couldn't believe it.

"Oh, the man said never to separate them, now I know why. Coco is helpless without Star, but when he is with Star, he can manage just fine," Don said.

The children were thrilled with the new horses and an hour later they were riding both horses around the yard. Coco was following Star as closely as if they were tied together with an invisible rope. I explained that Coco was blind and could only be ridden while he was walking behind Star. After watching long enough to make sure the horses were gentle and the children were in control, Don and I walked back toward the house.

From out of nowhere came the sound of hooves and a loud, "Whoopee, go Coco!" We turned back just in time to see Snow Cloud galloping across the meadow on Coco. My heart jumped inside of me as I pictured them crashing into a tree or falling into a ditch.

We began running after Snow Cloud but he suddenly turned Coco around and was racing toward us. Coco galloped past us and through the gate and into the corral. Snow Cloud pulled Coco to a stop and climbed off.

"That's a great horse!" he exclaimed.

"Snow Cloud, you could have been hurt!" I panted, "Coco can't see anything, he is blind."

"He doesn't have to see. I watch the trail for him, I would never take him any place dangerous or let him get hurt," Snow Cloud patted the horses neck, "He trusts me."

It was as simple as that. Coco was helpless and at the complete mercy of the other animals and people around him but he wasn't nervous or afraid. He trusted Star to lead him around the pasture and to the barn and to the water trough. He trusted Snow Cloud to guide him safely through the trees and along the trail. Coco, a small white horse had known us less than an hour but trusted us completely with his life.

I'd known God for years, but sometimes I didn't trust Him that much.

Trust is a blind horse running at breakneck speed with a young boy on his back. The boy trusting the horse to obey his every command instantly and the horse trusting his master to always do what was best for him. There was no room for a whisper of doubt or fear between them.

Over the next few years, Snow Cloud and Coco rode hundreds of miles together. Coco became a celebrity and people often stopped to watch Coco and his guide horse strolling around the pasture. Coco and Star were more than horses; they were friends, pets and teachers.

After ten happy years, Coco died. On a cold January morning

I walked into the barn to give the horses some hay and Coco was dead. He'd died in his sleep, without pain, without a struggle. He'd been fine the night before when he'd followed his old friend into the barn for the last time. Star stood silently beside his long time companion with his head down. I sat down beside Coco and cried. Coco had been a special gift. Now that he was gone we would all miss him terribly.

Freezing rain was falling while Lost Deer and I dug a grave for the horse. We chipped away at the rocky, frozen ground for six hours until we dug a grave big enough for our friend. Before we buried Coco, I cut off a lock of his white mane to keep. Years ago, when my own horse, Thunderhooves, died, I had taken a lock of the mane. I still had it in a little box. I'd kept it over 27 years and I still couldn't look at it without getting tears in my eyes.

We buried Coco and laid his bridle on the grave. Star stood a few feet away and whinnied as if his heart would break. Star mourned for weeks and we thought he'd die from grief. He paced along the fence all day looking for his friend. The goats seemed to sense Star's grief and adopted him. The goats followed him around all day and at night they slept curled up at his feet. He grew sleek and fat again and the children rode him all spring and summer but in the autumn, when the leaves turned brown and the first frost came, Star gave up. We found him laying only a few feet from Coco's grave. We buried him where we found him.

It broke our hearts.

Chapter Five

OAK LEAVES IN OCTOBER

When Little Antelope was twelve he was offered a summer job. It was easy; it only took fifteen minutes a day and paid well.

The only problem was, the woman who wanted to hire him was crazy. Everyone knew Miss Neal was crazy and people were afraid of her. I had to admit I'd heard some pretty strange stories about Miss Neal and wondered about my son's safety.

"Maybe we could go see Miss Neal together," I suggested. "We could decide for ourselves if she's…" I didn't want to use the word 'crazy', "If she's the kind of lady you want to work for."

Little Antelope was embarrassed to have his mother accompany him on his first job interview but he was also a little relieved he wouldn't have to face crazy Miss Neal all alone. We walked up the path to the old, two-story house where Miss Neal had spent her entire life.

The curtains were pulled shut and the windows were tightly closed, in spite of the summer heat.

We knocked on the door and a weak voice asked us to come inside. We found Miss Neal sitting in a rocking chair next to a wood stove. The room already felt like an oven but Miss Neal put another stick of wood into the small fire.

"I'm always cold," she explained, "You'll need to fill my wood box twice a week. Mostly I just want someone to come by every day to see if I'm still here or gone to Heaven."

Little Antelope moved his chair a couple of inches further away from the stove. The idea of coming here one day and finding Miss Neal's soul had gone to heaven but her body still here, didn't make this job sound any better.

I tried to look around the room without being snoopy. The house was barren. That is the word that stuck in my mind. Barren. There were no family pictures or keepsakes; there was none of the clutter that fills old ladies' homes.

She was ninety years old but, for all she owned, she could have been born yesterday. She'd collected nothing during her lifetime. She was dark and skinny, so skinny she looked like a bundle of sticks tied together in the shape of a person.

"You have nice hair, Little Antelope, but not as nice as Mark's. His hair is the color of oak leaves in October, there is no other way to describe it except oak leaves in October," she smiled and her face bunched up into happy wrinkles.

"I guess I don't know him," Little Antelope said, "No boy in school has hair that color."

"No, you wouldn't know him. He went away when he was seventeen. Mark and I were both born in 1900. He was born April fifteenth and I was born April eighteenth," she said. "We were sweethearts always. We were going to be married that summer in 1917 but World War I was going on and he had to go away."

The room was so silent I held my breath without knowing why.

"He hasn't come back yet, but he will. He wrote wonderful letters to me. The war was terrible, the German winter was bitter cold," she rocked back and forth, "Mark told me how cold it was and I was never warm again. Everyone has died, all of his family, all of my family, all of our friends. I'm the only one who will be here to welcome him back when the war is over."

I looked at my son and prayed he'd keep silent. "Don't tell her, please don't tell her," I prayed. He didn't. World War I might have ended in 1918 for other people but for Miss Neal it had raged on seventy-four years.

"Do you want the job?" she asked, "Some boys say they want the job but they never come back. They think I'm crazy. Do you think I'm crazy?"

"No. Well, maybe," Little Antelope answered, "But everybody is crazy in their own way. I'd like the job." She laughed, it was a gentle laugh and I knew my son had nothing to fear from her. "I'll start in the morning. My Dad has fresh strawberries, I could bring some to you," he offered.

"That would be nice but bring enough for two, will you?" she asked, "in case Mark comes home. He loves strawberries."

Little Antelope went to her house every morning all summer. He took her flowers and vegetables from our garden. When he forgot to pay him he just shrugged it off and said it didn't matter. Sometimes he took some pie or cake to her for a treat; he always took two pieces, just in case. For Little Antelope, World War I wasn't something in a dusty history book anymore. It was a terrible nightmare that could have happened yesterday because Miss Neal had lost her one true love when she was seventeen and spent the rest of her life alone and never felt warm again.

In September she had a stroke and was placed in a nursing home. She died soon afterwards.

She was the last person in the world to remember the color of Mark's hair the way it looked in 1917. It was the color of oak leaves in October and they were sweethearts always.

Chapter Six

NO SLEEP FOR ME TONIGHT

Nightmares can be terrifying. They sneak up on a child when they are asleep, pounce on their bed and wake them up, leaving them with pounding hearts. Suddenly, every shadow in the room looks like a monster.

Snow Cloud was having nightmares. Hardly a night passed that he didn't wake up and call out for me.

Sometimes telling a child he is safe isn't enough. Sometimes a child needs more.

I remembered the Dream Net. Almost every tribe has its own version of the dream net or catcher and mothers have used them for centuries to keep bad dreams away, promising their children the bad dreams will fly through the hole in the net.

I wanted my children to trust in God and not in superstition. Each night when the children finished their prayers, we repeated the promises in the Psalms.

"I will both lay me down in peace and sleep for thou Lord only makest me dwell in safety" (Psalm 4:8). "When thou liest down, thou shalt not be afraid: yea, thou shalt lie down and thy sleep shall be sweet," (Psalm 3:24).

I could plant the Word of God in the hearts of these tiny souls but sometimes children need something they can see and touch before they can believe.

Jesus understood this when Thomas needed to see and touch the wounds on Jesus before he could believe.

Snow Cloud needed more than words to feel safe.

"I think you are old enough to know the family secret," I whispered to Snow Cloud as I held him in my arms after a bad dream.

"Family secret?" Snow Cloud asked, his dark brown eyes sparkling with excitement.

"Yes, but you can't tell anyone else. Only two people can know this secret, just you and me," I warned.

"I won't tell," he whispered loudly enough for anyone to hear.

I took his hand in mine and we crept through the house until we stood at the front door.

"Here's the secret," I said, "This isn't any ordinary door. It is a genuine Bear Door. It was carved out of ironwood by an old man who lived far away in the mountains. There were hundreds of bears in the mountains and he knew he had to have the strongest door in the world. This door can keep out bears and wolves and bad people and nightmares."

Snow Cloud reached out and put his hands on the wooden door.

"As long as we have this Bear Door, nothing bad can ever come into our house. The biggest bear in the world couldn't break down this door but you are so strong, you can push it open with one finger," I said.

He opened the door and pushed it with one finger and then he looked at me and smiled.

"How do we know it can keep bears out?" he asked.

"Have you ever seen a bear in our kitchen?" I asked. "You know if a bear ever came into our house, the first place he would go is into the kitchen because he'd want to eat all of our food, especially my chocolate chip cookies. The first time we see a bear in the kitchen eating cookies, we'll know the door is old and worn out. Until then, the Bear Door is as strong as iron and will keep out all the bad things."

When he was older he would learn that Jesus was the door, just like in the Bible when Jesus said, "I am the door, by me, if any man enter in, he shall be saved…" (John 10:9).

The nightmares disappeared. Almost a year passed before Snow Cloud came to me and took my hand and led me to the door.

"Look at the door Mom, it has dents and scratches in it where I kick it open all the time. It's just a door," he laughed, "it's not a Bear Door and it's not carved out of ironwood. It is a cheap wooden door that couldn't keep a hungry butterfly out of the house. You made that up!"

"It kept out the nightmares," I reminded him.

"No . . . You kept out the nightmares," he said hugging me. "Thanks, Mom."

Chapter Seven

I USED TO BE TALLER

I used to be taller. At least I thought I was tall. I towered over my children like a giant oak tree. Now the children are growing so fast that some day they will be taller than I am. Every time I think I know who I am, somebody tells me I'm somebody else.

When I was a child, people told me I was a half-breed. I was half Indian and half White. Sometimes I wondered if there was a line drawn on my body somewhere that divided me into two different people. I was half of something and half of something else, but not a whole person. If I wore moccasins and beadwork, people would say I was trying too hard to be an Indian. If I wore dresses and curled my hair, I was told I was trying too hard to be White.

An old woman told me once I couldn't be Indian because my ears stuck out too much and all Indians had small ears that were close to their heads. A girl told me my nose was big and sharp and was an Indian nose because White people had small noses. My hair is dark, my skin is light, my nose is Indian, my ears are the ears of a White person. I always felt part of both races, but in my heart, if I leaned in one direction more than the other, then I felt I was more Indian.

Then people told me I wasn't an Indian; I was a Native American. There's nothing wrong with being a Native American and many people prefer to be known by that name. I was just raised as an Indian and I'm most comfortable with that name. I am not offended by it.

Then I was told I couldn't say I was half-White. I was half-Caucasian. Now I'm not a half-breed woman: I'm a racially mixed Native American and Caucasian person.

If someone asked me what my occupation was I would say I was a housewife. Wrong. I'm not married to a house. I'm a homemaker or a domestic engineer or a family manager.

Some people don't want to be called "mother" or "father" because they feel those names are biased and give a false image of male and female roles. (I think it is still all right to use the words male and female.) Some people prefer the term "parental unit." To me, that sounds like a computer or robot.

It took me a long time to learn to be proud of being a half-breed. I like being called an Indian. I don't mind being called a housewife, and I want my kids to call me Mom.

We live in an old farmhouse and we have a big tipi set up in the back yard. I have deer antlers and a buffalo skull hanging on the limbs of a dead tree. I love that old tipi and children and I spend a lot of time sitting in it and talking, but I don't want to live in it. I like living in a house and I like watching television and having modern conveniences, but that tipi is part of who I am and it will always sit in our yard like a big sign that says, "Crying Wind lives here."

Don is a White man who farms (Caucasian male agricultural engineer). Sometimes our cultures might overlap but they don't clash and we might not always understand each other but that isn't a problem.

When our children were born we gave them names that were both Indian and non-Indian. Our oldest son was named Aaron Troy Little Antelope; our second son was named Shane Travis Lost Deer; our third son was named Trinity Peter Snow Cloud; our daughter was named Spring Storm. I chose that name because it could be an Indian name or a non-Indian name. Don said I chose it because by the time she was born we were too broke to give her a longer name.

The children are comfortable with all of their names, which causes confusion sometimes for other people who aren't sure whether to call them "Shane" or "Lost Deer." Don uses their non-Indian names; I usually call them by their Indian names.

People often have trouble with my name, although most of my friends just call me "Cry"—short for Crying Wind. Sometimes people I've just met get mixed up and call me Flying Cloud, Crying Wolf and Singing Wind. It doesn't matter, I know who I am.

I'm an Indian.

Chapter Eight

THE RIVER

When I was six years old, my best friend drowned.

The river looked cold, black and bottomless. When they finally found my friend, people stood along the banks of the river and cried. I didn't cry because I thought my friend would come back tomorrow or next week and I saved some candy for us to share when my friend returned. I didn't know death meant forever.

A year later, I was riding in a car with my uncles when we drove across a bridge, which collapsed, and the car was plunged into the river. The car caught on some timbers that kept us from going completely underwater. But as I sat in the back seat, watching water pour in through the window, I was too paralyzed with fear to move even when a fish swam in, flopped across my lap and swam out the other window.

My uncle managed to get us all to safety and back to solid ground. While my uncles mourned the loss of the car, I looked into the black water and wondered if my friend's spirit was somehow still in the river. I couldn't imagine anything worse than being trapped in that horrible, dark, cold water.

When I grew up, I made a point of staying as far away from water as possible. I'd have been perfectly happy living in the middle of a desert where the only water could have been in my canteen.

When Don's boss was married, he invited us to the wedding reception at a beautiful hotel that had fountains and waterfalls in the lobby. Being a generous man, he also said we could bring our four children. Don and I agreed we'd each keep an eye on two of the children and we'd only stay one hour. That way the children wouldn't get bored or tired and we could leave before anyone saw what it was like to have four children under five years old. We both prayed for the happiness of the newlyweds and prayed the children wouldn't do anything to embarrass us. We didn't know we were praying for the wrong people.

I had a beautiful new dress with a long full skirt and Don had a new blue suit. We seldom had the clothes or the reason to dress up. We drank punch and ate cute little sandwiches. Just as the bride and groom were about to cut the cake, I looked across the lobby just in time to see two-year-old Spring Storm disappear into one of the fountain pools. She would drown!

I dropped my cup of punch and ran through the crowded lobby and jumped into the pool to save my daughter. The pool was only knee deep. I stood there soaking wet while my full skirt floated on the surface of the water like a wilted flower. To make things even more humiliating, Spring Storm hadn't actually been in the water. She'd been on the other side of the pool and it had only appeared she was in the water.

I climbed out of the pool, my skirt dripping gallons of water, my shoes sloshing like sponges and walked to the car while Don led the four children along behind me.

There was no point in trying to explain why a mature adult woman would run across a room and leap into a fountain. I was afraid everyone would think I was drunk. Or crazy.

The next day we decided it was time for everyone to learn how to swim. The four children learned in a matter of days. No matter how hard I tried, I couldn't overcome my fear of water. If someone threw a rock and me into the water at the same time, I would have sunk to the bottom first. In a family of swimmers, I'm the only one who sits on the shore and watches the others.

One day I was watching the children play in the creek when Snow Cloud swam farther than he ever had before. My mouth began to feel dry and my heart began to pound. I walked to the edge of the water and waved for him to come back but he didn't hear me. He was too far; he'd never make it back to shore. I looked around; everyone else was too far away to reach him.

"Come back! Come back!" I called. Tears were running down my cheeks. He wouldn't make it. He'd never make it. He'd drown! Snow Cloud disappeared under the water. There was no time. I ran and plunged into the water. "Please God!" I prayed, "Let me swim for three minutes, just three minutes out of my whole life!"

I'd heard stories about people who'd never been able to swim and then they'd saved someone from drowning. I'd heard of people who had super-human strength for just a few minutes and lifted cars off people and saved them from being crushed. I could do it! I could swim out and save my son from drowning!

No, I couldn't.

I moved my arms and I kicked my legs and I sank to the bottom faster than a rock and stayed there. I was going to die. I was going to drown just like my best friend had died so long ago. I looked around me. Far away I could see Snow Cloud's legs kicking in the water. He would make it; he'd be safe. I was going to die. What a stupid way to die. I was out of air. I couldn't hold my breath any longer.

Something grabbed my hair and yanked me upward. I was headed toward the surface. I might make it! I burst onto the surface of the water like a beaching whale. Lost Deer dragged me up by my hair and was pulling me toward the bank of the creek.

"Snow Cloud!" I choked on the water.

"He's fine, he's already on shore," Lost Deer said. "Don't you ever do that again, Mom. I saw you running toward the water and I yelled and told you not to jump in but you jumped anyway. Please, Mom, stop saving us before you kill yourself."

That was the last time I jumped into the water.

I don't know why God answers some prayers and not others. I thought it was a good idea for God to let me swim three minutes to save my son. I guess He thought it was a better idea for me not to jump into the water in the first place.

Two of my favorite people in the Bible are Thomas and Peter. I can sympathize with both of them. Doubting Thomas, who had to see Jesus' wounds before he could believe, and Peter, who sometimes believed too quickly and then had doubts later which left him all wet. Still, Thomas and Peter showed a lot of courage. Thomas wanted to believe: he just wanted to be sure what he believed was true. Considering all the false prophets running around it seemed smart to be careful.

Peter was a fisherman, he'd lived beside the sea all his life and he knew for a fact you can't walk on water. When Jesus commanded him to "Come," Peter immediately climbed out of the boat and walked on the water. The water he walked on was dark and deep and he must have been afraid but he walked. Peter might have sunk but none of the other disciples even got out of the boat.

If we don't question and don't doubt, how can we grow? If our faith is too fragile to withstand close examination, maybe we have put our faith in the wrong place. If we have questions God can't answer, then our God is too small. Maybe it shows greater faith to question than to blindly believe.

Just as my children ask questions about the things they don't understand, I ask God, "Why? When? How?" God always has more answers than I have questions.

Chapter Nine

THE PRICE OF LOVE

I've lost my marbles!" I gasped. I kept five marbles in a glass jar on the bookshelf and now they were gone. "Who has my marbles?"

"Lost Deer is playing with them in the yard," Little Antelope said, "What difference does it make? They are just old marbles."

"They are worth more than gold," I said. "They were a special gift from a friend a long time ago." We joined Lost Deer outside where he was playing in the sand with the marbles.

"Let me tell you the story about these marbles and why I've kept them since I was a little girl and why they mean so much to me," I said as the children stretched out on the grass in the shade of the apple tree. "It all started on a hot, summer day almost 100 years ago" I began.

"The Kansas sun blazed down on the little boy's sweat streaked face, his bare feet kicked up small puffs of dust as he hurried along the crooked dirt road. It was the summer of 1902 and five-year-old Loren Mendall was buying a bride. His right hand was shoved deep into the pocket of his faded overalls and his dirty fingers tightly gripped five marbles, two blues, two reds and a brown one with a chip in it.

"Loren was an orphan who lived with a family down by the railroad tracks. They had seven kids of their own, and Loren was given the leftovers. He was skin and bones, and people nicknamed him "Buckshot" because his clothes were so ragged they looked like they'd been shot full of holes.

"Minnie stood on the porch of her three-story mansion waiting for him. Her black hair was in tight little curls and her plump, pink cheeks were always dimpled from her smile. When she saw Loren, she waved and ran across the yard to meet him.

"'Daddy is in the garden,' she said and led the way to the back yard. Loren took a deep breath and walked up to the tall, thin man picking tomatoes.

"Minnie's father owned the newspaper as well as the largest store in town and many pieces of property. He was very rich and very important. Minnie was his only child. Minnie could have anything she wanted and she wanted Loren, the little boy with the crooked smile she'd met in the park.

"'Daddy, I want you to meet Loren,' she was almost dancing with excitement, 'He has something to tell you.'

"Mr. Crowder placed his tomatoes in his basket and turned to look at the two children. There stood his precious Minnie, looking as delicate as a china doll in her white lace dress, and next to her was a pathetic little boy, his feet caked with dirt, half-starved and so filthy he smelled bad. 'What do you want to tell me?' Mr. Crowder asked.

"'I'm here to marry Minnie and I'll pay you five marbles for her,' Loren said. Minnie's heart pounded and she felt dizzy. Her eyes pleaded with her daddy and her chin began to tremble.

"'Let's see the marbles.' Mr. Crowder held out his hand and Loren placed them in his big palm, one at a time.

"He started to place the brown one, chipped side down, but instead he said, 'This one is chipped, but it still rolls good.'

"'It is a pleasure to meet an honest man,' Mr. Crowder said and looked at the marbles carefully. 'These are fine marbles, do you have any more?'

"'No, sir. That is all I own,' Loren answered, his voice fading a little.

"'If you are willing to give all you own for my daughter, then I guess that is enough.' He looked at Minnie who was holding her breath, 'How do you feel about it?'

"'I want to marry him, Daddy,' she said, shaking her curls.

"'I guess it is settled, then. Loren, you can marry my daughter, but her Mama would cry if she left home now and Minnie needs a nice house to live in. You wait until she is grown up and build her a house, then we'll talk about a wedding.' He dropped the marbles into his pocket and went back to his garden. Minnie and Loren ran into the front yard and hid under the lilac bush.

They were getting married! Daddy said it was all right! They drew plans for their house in the dirt and used rocks and twigs for furniture.

"That evening, Mr. Crowder told his wife their five-year-old Minnie had been spoken for and they had a good laugh. He placed the marbles in the bottom drawer of a desk where they stayed for twelve years. Minnie and Loren remained best friends in spite of everyone's efforts to discourage them. Minnie refused to have a birthday party unless Loren was invited and Loren made countless trips to her house, bringing her wildflowers and bird nests and anything else he found that he thought she might like.

"When Loren turned thirteen, Mr. Crowder gave him a job in one of his stores and found an older couple who took him into their house where he was given good food and warm clothing for the first time in his life.

"When Loren turned sixteen, Mr. Crowder made him an assistant manager in his store, explaining how Loren had been honest with him when it might have cost him everything he wanted.

"'I can trust a boy like that,' he said. 'He doesn't even know who his parents are but they had to be good people because I've never seen a more honest boy.' Loren had a job and began to date Minnie.

"In the spring of 1914, at the age of seventeen, Loren and Minnie were married. Minnie's wedding gown was the most elegant anyone had ever seen in the Kansas town. It was like a cloud of white satin and lace. Minnie stepped gracefully down the aisle carrying her bouquet of pink roses and wildflowers, and tucked into the bouquet was a tiny satin bag holding the five marbles Loren had given to Mr. Crowder twelve years earlier.

"Minnie and Loren had three sons, two daughters, and twenty-one grandchildren. They were married sixty-one years and the marbles were kept in a crystal bowl on their mantle.

"It was a tradition in the Mendal family for the men to give five marbles to the women they loved. It was a pledge that they were willing to give all they owned for their love. Eight brides carried wedding bouquets with a secret tucked in the bridal bouquet, a tiny lace bag holding five marbles, two blue, two red and one brown one with a chip in it."

The children were silent for a minute while they thought about the story. "But Mom, how did you get the marbles?" Lost Deer asked as he placed the marbles in my hand.

"A boy gave them to me a long time ago, he was the great-great grandson of Loren and Minnie," I said. "We were very young but we were in love the way only children can be. We promised to grow up and get married someday."

"What happened to him?" Spring Storm asked.

"He died," I said but couldn't say more. I held the marbles in my hand, remembering the day a little boy had given me all he had and I wondered what would have happened if he hadn't drowned when he was six.

Chapter Ten

THE DRY WELL

I was the accidental offspring of two people who hated each other. "Never again!" were the first words I heard in this world and they were spoken by my mother at the moment of my birth. She told Shima Sai, my grandmother, that she hated two things in this world: children and dogs but if she had to choose one of them she'd choose the dog because you can always shoot a dog.

My father had abandoned my mother as soon as she discovered she was pregnant. My mother blamed me for ruining her life and abandoned me.

At times I was passed around from relatives to neighbors like a gift nobody wants and finally my grandmother and my uncles raised me.

I grew up feeling unwanted, worthless and ugly. I longed for parents and a mother's tender love. I would cut pictures of people out of books and pretend they were my "real" parents. I would carry the pictures around with me until the paper was wrinkled and torn, then I would search through books for a picture of new parents. It didn't matter to me what age or race or nationality they were, if they looked kind and gentle and if they were smiling, I would adopt them for a while.

When I had my own children I made sure the first words they heard in this world were, "I love you."

When my children asked why they didn't have grandparents like their friends did, it was hard to give them an answer.

I began searching for my parents and finally located them. I wrote them letters and sent them pictures of my children and myself and tried to arrange a meeting. My father never answered my letters. My mother said she didn't want to be reminded of her past mistakes and to please not write to her again. It was as if for years I'd taken a bucket and walked to a well for a cool drink of water. The well had always been dry and I hadn't been able to get one drop of water from the well in my entire life, but every single day, I would pick up my bucket and return to the well, hoping for, and expecting to find water. I would lower my bucket and pull it back up and when I found it was still empty, I'd cry or become angry and hurt and I'd walk home, hating the well for not filling my bucket and giving me what I wanted and needed.

At last, I realized the fault was not the well. The fault was mine. The well couldn't help being empty. People can't give what they don't have but I can stop running to a dry well. My parents never loved me and never will. Nothing I can do will ever change that. Sometimes the best and bravest thing we can do is give up and let go. We can't make people love us no matter how hard we try or how much we want their love.

God doesn't think I am an accident or a mistake. I never come away from God with an empty bucket; He always fills my heart with so much love that it overflows.

Chapter Eleven

THAT AWFUL MRS. ROONEY

That awful Mrs. Rooney has let her dogs out again!" I glared out of the window as the five hounds raced across the pasture and headed straight for our house. Our cats were already climbing the trees to escape the pack of drooling, floppy-eared, big-footed dogs.

Mrs. Rooney lived down the road from us and had recently started raising raccoon-hunting dogs. I didn't mind when the dogs howled at the full moon, in fact, it sort of reminded me of the days back on the reservation when the coyotes would howl at the moon all night. I didn't mind when her dogs used the deep hollows on our farm as a shortcut. What I did mind was when they came into our yard, stole the food from our pets and scared our cats so badly they'd spend the rest of the day perched on tree limbs. I was also worried about the way Freckles, the ugliest of the hounds, looked at our dog.

We had a beautiful female collie named Lucky, and the last

71

thing we wanted was a litter of puppies that were half collie and half-speckled hound.

Freckles leaped over the fence just as I grabbed Lucky and locked her in the barn. I chased the hounds away but not before they'd stolen the cat food and broken the bowl of milk I'd just put out for the cats.

I'd never met that awful Mrs. Rooney but we'd already started a feud that would probably last for years and involve our great-grandchildren. I'd called several times asking her if she'd call me when she was turning her dogs loose to run so that I could lock our dog in the barn until her dogs returned home. She always apologized for forgetting and promised she'd call me the next time. She never did.

In the meantime, at least twice a week, I found myself cleaning up something her dogs had broken or spilled. One day they grabbed some laundry off my clothesline and dragged it across the yard. I had to gather it up and wash and bleach it to get the muddy paw prints out of the sheets. I like dogs, but if they misbehave, I usually blame their owners. In this case I blamed that awful Mrs. Rooney.

When I found a tunnel dug under the barn, I knew Freckles had outsmarted us. When Lucky produced six of the ugliest puppies I'd ever seen there was no doubt that Freckles was their father.

I waited until the puppies were weaned then I tied red bows around their necks, put them in a box and headed to Mrs.

Rooney's house. I knocked on her door and shoved the box of wiggling puppies into her arms.

"I believe these belong to you," I said and walked away. I'd certainly taught that awful Mrs. Rooney a lesson! I'd been angry with her for weeks, no, for months, and now I had my revenge. The puppies were her problem and she'd have to take care of them until she found homes for them. Revenge was sweet. So why didn't getting even feel as good as I thought it would?

By the time I reached home I had to admit that I'd been small, petty and spiteful. I hate it when that happens. How could I have been so self-righteous? I'd made a fool out of myself, acted like a witch and I had no one to blame but myself. I was not the person I thought I was. God must be frowning and tapping his foot. I'd have to try to undo the damage I'd done but if I went back to her house, Mrs. Rooney would probably shoot me. No doubt about it. I was the most wretched, hateful human being on the face of the earth.

I'd bake a cake and take it to her and apologize and offer to take back three puppies and find homes for them. That was fair. Maybe she wouldn't shoot me. Maybe I'd stop feeling so mean. Maybe God would stop tapping his foot.

I baked a chocolate cake and was putting the last swirl of frosting on it when there was a knock on the door. It was that awful Mrs. Rooney. She'd come to kill me.

"I came to apologize for all the trouble I've caused you and to give you this casserole as a peace offering," she smiled, "I've also found homes for all six puppies."

"Please, come in, Mrs. Rooney," I said. "I just baked a cake for you. I was coming over to apologize and to try to convince you that I was temporarily insane when I brought the puppies to you."

"Please don't call me Mrs. Rooney, that's too formal. You can call me Holly," she paused, "My first name is really Polly but I like Holly better so that's the name I use."

"Your name is Polly Holly Rooney?" I choked back a giggle.

"I know, it's a terrible name. I was named after both of my grandmothers. I used to get teased a lot in school. I'm forty years old and I still get teased about my name," she smiled and shrugged. "Do I have to call you Mrs. Stafford or do you have a first name?"

"My name is Crying Wind," I said.

"You have to be kidding; you are named after a weather report?" she asked.

"It's an Indian name," I explained. "My friends call me Cry, for short."

"Cry? That sounds sad—maybe I can think up a nickname for you," she said.

"Do you have children?" I asked, curious what she would name them.

"I have a son but he is grown and lives in New Jersey," she said.

"What's his name?"

"Joe," she said, "It was the simplest name I could think of . . . I didn't want him to get teased in school like I was and I didn't think anyone could tease a kid about being named Joe. What are the names of your kids?"

This didn't seem like a good time to tell her about Little Antelope, Lost Deer, Snow Cloud and Spring Storm, so I changed the subject. "Let me put on some coffee and we'll try some of this casserole and have a piece of cake," I said.

We spent the next two hours talking and laughing. We'd both grown up in poverty and had been raised by people other than our parents. We found so many things we had in common it was as if we were twins, an Indian woman from Colorado and an Italian woman from New Jersey. We'd known each other for two hours. We'd known each other forever.

When Don came home from work I couldn't wait to tell him the news. "I met Mrs. Rooney today," I said.

"That awful Mrs. Rooney?" he asked.

"Don't you dare call her that! Holly Polly is the best friend I've ever had in my life," I said and took her casserole out of the oven. "Really, Don, you have to try to be more friendly to people."

He mumbled something but I didn't understand it, then he changed the subject. "Do you think you could find something to do with all of the cucumbers?" he asked. "The garden has a bumper crop; we're going to have hundreds, maybe even thousands of cucumbers."

It was the first time his garden had ever produced a big crop of anything. I wished it had been potatoes, you can do so much with potatoes. There isn't much you can do with cucumbers.

I was wrong. You can get into all sorts of trouble with a thousand cucumbers.

When Holly came over the next morning to return the cake dish she noticed the baskets of cucumbers sitting on the porch. "It would be a shame to waste all those cucumbers," she said, "I have an idea . . . "

At that moment something important happened but I didn't realize it at the time. Every time Holly would run her fingers through her black curly hair and say the words, "I have an idea . . ." it usually meant we were about to have an adventure. Not always a good one.

"I have an idea . . . let's make pickles. We can make enough to last us all winter," she said as she dug through the baskets of cucumbers like they were gold coins.

"Pickles? That sounds like a lot of work," I said doubtfully. It was July and at least 100 degrees outside. I didn't want to be trapped in a hot kitchen making pickles.

"I have a wonderful recipe for making pickles," she bubbled enthusiastically. "My mother gave it to me, her mother gave it to her. It's been in our family for a hundred years—it's our family's world famous secret recipe. I'll go to the store to get what we need and we can start this morning."

Holly is like that . . . she sort of sneaks up on you and leaves you spinning like a tornado before you even know what hit you. That day Holly and I made fifty quarts of pickles.

"I guarantee these will be the best pickles you've ever tasted in your life," she promised as we carried twenty-five quarts out to her car and loaded them into the trunk. "My mother never got around to trying this recipe herself but she got it from my grandmother who got it from her neighbor in Italy who said they were the best pickles in the world."

"Do you mean we made fifty quarts of pickles from a recipe you've never tasted?" I asked.

"Well, I've always wanted to make pickles but I just never got around to it. You know, the way your garden is growing, we could probably can another fifty quarts of pickles and sell them to that country store in Pineville and make some extra money," she said.

"If the recipe is as good as you say it is, you could even sell the recipe to some big company and make a fortune," I'd been inhaling vinegar fumes too long and was starting to think like Holly. "You could be a millionaire!"

"You mean we could be millionaires: we're partners in the pickle business. We could be the pickle queens of the world." Her eyes glazed over. "We'll be filthy rich and split everything fifty-fifty. We'll call our company Crying Polly Holly . . . or maybe Rooney-Wind . . . well, we'll have to work on the name," she said and drove away.

After she left I cleaned the kitchen and thought about our wonderful pickles and how rich we'd be. She was a great friend. Imagine having a gold mine like this and sharing it with me!

Twenty-five jars of pickles were lined up in the cupboard. Our fortune. Our fame. Our future. I couldn't wait to let the family taste them. They'd be so proud of me and Don would be thrilled that his farm had finally produced something that would make us rich.

At dinner I placed a big bowl of pickles in the center of the table. I'd let everyone taste them first and after they raved about how delicious they were, I'd break the news to them about my new business.

"Ugh! I think I'm going to be sick!" Spring Storm gagged.

"These are the worst pickles I've ever tasted," Little Antelope said. "What's wrong with them?"

"I think my teeth are melting." Snow Cloud gulped some water.

"They're pretty bad," Don said. "You should take them back to the store and complain. Maybe you can get your money back."

"There's nothing wrong with these pickles!" I grabbed one and bit into it. "They're deelishious . . . thersh noshink glong sush zem." My tongue had shriveled up.

"Some people like sour pickles," Don said. "Was there any kind of warning on the label about these being extra, extra super sour?"

"At least we only have one jar to get rid of," Snow Cloud said.

I drank two glasses of water and changed the subject. I didn't know whether to call Holly and warn her that we'd made the world's worst pickles or to keep quiet. What if they were supposed to be this sour and her family loved them? I didn't want to hurt her feelings. I decided not to say anything but tomorrow I'd have to get rid of the pickles.

I didn't have to wait long. Some boys from church came after dinner and asked if we had any canned goods we could donate to the Daily Bread project. The church often collected food and clothing to give to struggling families and anyone was welcome to come to the church to get a box of food.

I went to the kitchen and filled a sack with cans of vegetables. When I opened the cupboard I stared at the pickles. There was nothing wrong with them except they were really, really sour.

Just because we didn't like them didn't mean someone else wouldn't like them. The Bible said to give generously because your gifts would return to you later. Surely giving the pickles to someone was better than throwing them away and wasting food. I helped the boys carry out a sack of canned goods and twenty-four jars of pickles and loaded them into the church van. It was for the best. My family wouldn't have to eat pickles they didn't like and Holly wouldn't have her pride hurt and some lucky person would get a zillion pickles.

I'd invited Holly to visit our church any time she felt like it but I was surprised to see her at church on Sunday. The minister welcomed the congregation and then made his announcements that the Daily Bread project was a big success and they'd collected twice as much food as they'd hoped for.

"We were given many, many boxes of canned goods and forty-eight quarts of home made pickles," the minister said. He was wrong. I'd only given him twenty-four quarts. I suddenly gasped and leaned forward in the pew and looked at Holly. She was staring at me.

It was obvious. We'd each had twenty-five jars of pickles, we'd each opened one jar, hated the way they tasted, and then each gave the rest of the jars to the church. We both started to laugh. We were on the road to a wonderful friendship. We became so close that at Christmas we bought each other the same gift.

She gave up raising hound dogs, which I have to admit, made me very happy, but she was always looking for a new way to get rich. In the time I knew her she started a dozen businesses and failed at them all. She always managed to survive and never lost her sense of humor.

Tuesday was our day to spend together. We shopped or cooked or cleaned or painted or worked in our yards or rode horses. It didn't matter what we did as long as we did it together. We'd finish each other's sentences, laugh at each other's jokes (no matter how often we'd heard them) and sympathize over each other's problems. But mostly we laughed together, somehow, when we were together, everything seemed funny.

I've had some wonderful friends in my life but I've never had another friend quite like Polly Holly Rooney. She was one of a kind.

Chapter Twelve

THE TRUTH HURTS

My friend is dying. Polly Holly Rooney has cancer and I've been watching her slip slowly away for months.

At first she had complained about just being tired. She was caught somewhere between never really feeling sick and never really feeling well. She tried changing her diet and taking vitamins but it didn't help and finally she went to the doctor for tests. When she didn't like the results of the tests she went to a different doctor and took more tests but the second set of tests came back with the same results. She had cancer, it was running through her body like a wildfire.

We both cried and then we prayed and then we decided to fight back. We both read everything we could find about cancer and for awhile, the future looked promising. Some people lived long lives with hardly any symptoms at all, sometimes the cancer would just disappear and never come back.

Holly decided to try everything, she went into health food and vitamins in a big way, she attended church more and read her Bible and asked for prayers. She wanted her body and her soul to be in top condition.

She also followed her doctor's advice and took her medication. After all, how could a small thing like cancer beat someone like Polly Holly?

Polly seemed to improve for a few months, she had more energy, she looked better, she was talking about her future and making jokes about what a couple of ugly old ladies we were going to be. I told her I didn't mind getting old and ugly because I knew I'd have a best friend who was old and ugly, too.

Then, one day, she said she was feeling a little worse and the doctor said she should check into the hospital for a few days so he could keep an eye on her and run some more tests.

I visited her every day and brought balloons and flowers and magazines. I caught her up on the local gossip and brushed her hair, which had become thin and dry, trying hard not to pull it because her scalp was so tender. Holly's beautiful, thick, black hair, was dull and lifeless, it broke off easily and I was always careful not to let her see how much of her hair came off in the brush. Her once sparkling brown eyes now looked shadowed and sad. I hardly recognized her.

"You're looking better today, there is more color in your cheeks and you seem stronger," I said, "At this rate you'll be out of here before Christmas. There's a new store in the mall and it has the most beautiful things and the prices are so low that everything is practically free! We'll go there as soon as you feel up to it."

"Okay," Holly smiles, "What else will we do?"

"Well, we'll sit for days at a time and gossip and eat ice cream and get as fat as cows," I said and I saw the pain in her eyes. "What's wrong, Holly? Are you hurting? Should I get a nurse?"

"No, I'm fine," tears made her eyes shiny.

I grabbed a tissue and gently blotted her tears away. Her skin looked as thin and delicate as the tissue I was holding.

"Tell me what's going on, Holly," I pleaded but she ignored me. I remembered a game I used to play when I was a kid and said, "A penny for your thoughts and you have to tell me the truth."

I took a penny out of my purse and placed it in her hand.

Her thin fingers wrapped around it and she gave a small laugh.

"Oh, Cry, I haven't heard anyone say that for years . . . a penny for your thoughts . . . it sounds so good. I wish we could go back to being children again, life was so simple then. Remember when all we had to do all summer long was decide which dolls we were going to play with and what kind of candy we'd buy with our allowance? I wish life was like that now," she sighed.

"I do too, believe me, I wish we could turn back the clock but when we were kids all we wanted to do was grow up. Now we are all grown up and it isn't what we expected it to be," I agreed, "But you're stalling, I paid you a genuine copper penny for your thoughts and you haven't told me the truth."

"I want to go home. I don't want to spend any more time lying in a hospital bed watching tubes drip fluid into my arm while other tubes collect my urine. Let's face it, I'm pretty disgusting to be around. I spray on too much perfume before anyone comes, trying to cover up the smell of the medicine and antiseptics. I don't want anyone's pity, especially not yours!" Holly sniffed.

I swallowed and tried to choose my words carefully so I didn't make her feel worse.

"As soon as you get out of the hospital . . . "

A nurse came in and gave Holly a pill, took her temperature and checked her pulse.

I stepped into the hallway to give them some privacy. While I was waiting, I saw Doctor Martinez and hurried down the hall to catch him.

"Hi," I fell into step beside him, "I think Holly looks a little better today, don't you? Will she be able to go home in time for Christmas?"

He stopped and looked deep into my eyes.

"I think we'd better have a talk," he led me to a small office and we sat down beside each other on a black sofa.

"There is no easy way to say this, but Holly isn't doing well at all. She's getting weaker every day. I'm sorry, your friend is not going to last much longer," he said as gently as he could. "You can't be surprised, you know her body is riddled with cancer, you've seen her get weaker and weaker."

"But she has color in her cheeks, she looks better and she's not in as much pain as she was . . . " I argued.

"She has color in her cheeks because she is flushed with a fever, we've increased her medication so she doesn't feel the pain. She's fairly comfortable right now, we have the vomiting and pain under control but we haven't stopped the cancer, it's raging in her body . . . " he said.

I gasped at the word. I'd thought of cancer as a slow, almost lazy disease, but when he said it was raging through her body it sounded like a fire burning up her life.

"What can we do? Maybe some new medicine, chemo-therapy?" I pleaded, "There must be something else we can do!"

"We've done everything we can. The type of cancer she has is brutal, she's lasted longer than most. All we can do is keep her from suffering," he shook his head, "I'd give anything if we could save her. She is such a nice woman, she could have still given so much to life, I'm so sorry."

"How much time does she have?" I asked and gave up fighting the tears and just let them roll down my cheeks.

"It's hard to put cancer on a time table, sometimes you expect a person to live a year and they die a week later. The opposite is also true, I've had patients I thought would die in a few days and they lasted months . . . " he said, "but Holly, I'd guess she has a few weeks."

"Weeks!" I choked, "Weeks? I want her to live years, not weeks!"

"Well, she has a lot to live for, she has friends who love her, you always cheer her up when you visit, she has her son. All these things help her hold on to life," he said.

"Has her son contacted you? Does he know?" I asked.

"She told me she'd taken care of it. I don't think he has called, I know he hasn't been here to visit. Some people can't watch a loved one suffer, that doesn't make them bad, I'm not even sure it makes them weak. We all have our limits, don't be too hard on him, I've seen it happen a thousand times, people can't handle the truth so they hide from it," he said gently.

I wiped my tears away and followed him back into Holly's room. I put a smile on my face and did my best to look cheerful.

"Aha!" Holly said, "I knew the two of you were talking about me behind my back!"

"You know I'm a happily married man," Dr. Martinez said, "But if I wasn't, you'd be the first woman I asked for a date."

Holly smiled at him. She trusted him completely, he'd taken care of her for months. She thought he was going to cure her.

The next day I went to the hospital early and a nurse was still in the room with Holly.

"Look, Holly ate a whole bowl of cherry gelatin! She's going to get fat," the nurse said, proudly holding up the empty bowl that had probably held two ounces of gelatin.

"Yeah, I think she's gained at least a pound," I agreed. "Pretty soon you'll get so fat you'll roll right out of bed."

I looked at her thin arms and wondered if she even weighed a hundred pounds. Dear God! What if this was the last time we were together and our last conversation was about cherry gelatin!

"Did you watch TV last night?" Holly asked, "This man had a parrot on the show that could say three hundred words, except that it wouldn't talk. I think the bright lights scared him."

We were all talking about nonsense, we pretended Holly wasn't in a hospital bed, we acted like we were sitting home in the living room and everything was fine.

After the nurse left, Holly asked me to paint her fingernails thinking it might lift her spirits.

"How do you like the color?" I asked, "It's called Hawaiian sunset."

"I wish I could have seen a Hawaiian sunset," she said sadly.

"Maybe you'll go to Hawaii someday," I said and kept painting her nails.

She reached for something on the night stand.

"A penny for your thoughts . . . and you have to tell the truth," she said and handed me the penny I'd given her the day before.

I looked at the tarnished copper coin and slipped it into my coat pocket.

"What's the question?" I asked.

"Am I going to die?" she asked calmly.

"Everybody dies," I said.

"You're being silly. You know what I mean. The nurse tells me I'm getting fat, you tell me I'm looking better, the doctor tells me to keep a positive outlook, the minister tells me to pray for a miracle," she said, "If you were the one lying in this bed and I was the one standing there, I'd tell you the truth." She blinked back tears, "Please tell me the truth."

I couldn't lie to her anymore, I loved her too much. I took her small hand in mine.

"I'm sorry, I don't think you have much time left." I was surprised my voice sounded normal. "You won't be able to go home for Christmas."

"Will I still be alive at Christmas?" she asked.

"I don't know, no one knows. The doctor says a lot of it is up to you, wanting to live can add time to your life but eventually the cancer will win. He said you wouldn't be in any pain, he'd make sure you were comfortable right up to the last," I said.

"Thank you for telling me the truth," she said, "I think I already knew I was getting weaker every day but no one would be honest."

"I know, we all kept hoping. Today when I heard the nurse talking about gelatin I wanted to scream. We've been wasting too much time playing games. It's time we stopped wasting time and started being honest. I think you need to call your son and tell him the truth and ask him to come and say goodbye."

"I haven't told him how sick I am. I didn't want to worry him. I want to see him . . . I love him," she choked on the words. "Oh, Cry, I don't want to die!"

We held each other and cried until there weren't any tears left. At that moment I would have traded a year of my life if I could have added a year of life to hers. If any kind of transplant had been possible I'd have gladly given her anything I had just to buy her one more year.

At last she lay back on her pillow, tired but somehow stronger.

"I have so much to do. Will you help me?" she asked.

"I'd do anything in the world for you," I promised.

"Then get a pen and paper and let's start a list. I want to write a letter to everyone I love, my son Joe of course, and you and some other friends and my cousins in Kansas. I want to tell all of you how much you meant to me and how much I love you and that you shouldn't mourn for me. I want everyone to go on with their lives, not waste one single day."

A tear slipped out of my eye and fell on the paper, making the ink run.

"I want to plan my own funeral because Joe will spend too much money and I know he can't afford it. I want something simple and I want to pick out what I'll wear, and I want to be cremated" she sniffed, "I want to talk to Joe and tell him how much he meant to me and how happy he made me. I want to tell him it's okay to sell all my stuff and my house and use the money for anything he wants and not to be sad or have any regrets, he was a perfect son. I want to write my own will . . ."

We both started crying again but there was also a healing in it. This was the right thing to do, it was hard now but it would make her death easier for her and for everyone else if she had the opportunity to tie up loose ends and take care of unfinished business. This way, there would be no regrets for her or anyone else.

Over the next few days I helped Holly write letters to everyone on her list. We ended up writing over thirty letters. I promised I would mail them after she was gone.

She told me she wanted to be cremated and have her ashes scattered in the hills behind her house where she used to spend so much time enjoying the pine trees and wild flowers.

Dr. Martinez was upset with me for being honest with Holly. He was afraid I'd taken away her hope and she'd give up and die sooner. But the opposite was true. Holly seemed to be happier and more at peace like a terrible burden had been lifted.

Of course, the worst part was finally facing the truth with her son. Both Holly and Joe had been in denial for a long time, desperately clinging to any thread of hope. It nearly broke Joe's heart to hear his mother talking about dying but he knew the last thing he could ever do for his mother was to help her face the days ahead with courage and love.

Joe flew home from New Jersey and they moved to a deeper level in their relationship. Even though they both knew they didn't have a future together, they talked about happy times in the past, sometimes they'd laugh and sometimes they'd cry. They knew even though they'd been cheated out of a long life together they'd still been lucky to have loved each other for the time they had.

I remembered how Holly had wished she could have gone to Hawaii and I arranged for a fantasy trip to the islands. I hung posters of palm trees and beaches in her room and got some tapes of Hawaiian music. I insisted everyone wear straw hats and sunglasses and flower leis. I wore a grass skirt and tried to do the hula. We all laughed until our sides ached. I gave Holly a lei of orchids and even after it wilted she kept it hanging on her bedpost.

"Thank you for my trip to Hawaii," she said after everyone else had left, "You've given me everything I could have ever wanted. None of this would have been possible if you hadn't been honest with me. I'd have spent my last days talking about cherry gelatin and wasting precious time. I'm so glad I got to say goodbye to everyone and tell them how much I loved them. I'm happy knowing Joe understands that I loved him with all my heart and I want him to live a full, rich life and have a house full of kids. It makes me feel good knowing my ashes will be scattered in a place I love so much and had so many good times in the past. Thanks for respecting me and loving me enough to tell me the truth."

"It was one of the hardest things I've ever had to do in my life," I admitted, "But I hope when my time comes someone will love me enough to tell me the truth so I can tie up loose ends and make things easier for those I love."

Holly died a week after we'd had the Hawaiian party. She slipped away quietly in her sleep.

A few friends, along with Joe and I, took her ashes up to the hills. Joe scattered her ashes in a grove of pines. I felt my heart had been ripped in half. She'd been my closest friend for six years. I didn't know how I could bear the grief I was feeling, how I could get through life without my best friend.

I reached into my coat pocket for a handkerchief to wipe my tears when my fingers wrapped about a coin.

I pulled it out and recognized the penny Holly had given me. I could almost hear her saying, "A penny for your thoughts . . . and you have to tell the truth." I smiled. She wasn't gone, not really, Holly was always going to be with all of us. I could almost feel her standing beside me, could almost see her smile. Someday we'd be together again. I knew it, because it wasn't a coincidence that I found the penny. It was a message from Holly and that's the truth.

A week later, Joe came to see me and brought two small

boxes of things Holly had left to me in her will. Joe said she'd left instructions that I was to open the larger box first and then the small box, because the most valuable thing was in the little box.

I opened the larger box first. She'd left me some photographs of the two of us, her favorite ring, some personal keepsakes and an antique vase that had belonged to her grandmother.

In the second box, tied up with a big red ribbon, was the family world famous secret recipe for Rooney-Wind Pickles.

I could almost hear her laughing.

Chapter Thirteen

DON IS GETTING OLDER

It was a shock when I first noticed that Don, my husband, was getting gray hair. No, that isn't true. It wasn't gray, it was white. He had six white hairs above his left ear. He was getting old!

I ran to the mirror and checked my hair. So far, so good. No white hair but it was just a matter of time—after all, we had four teenaged children—everyone knew that nothing gave you white hair faster than having teenagers in the house.

I didn't want to say anything to Don because I didn't want to upset him but it seemed like I couldn't even look at his face anymore; every time he walked into the room my eyes went straight to those white hairs.

I decided to save him the heartbreak of growing old. I waited until he was asleep and then I sneaked up, tweezers in hand, grabbed a hair and jerked it out of his head.

Don woke up with a loud roar. "A bee just stung me!" he shouted, waving his arms around in the air.

I hadn't expected him to wake up: usually he sleeps like a rock.

He saw me holding the tweezers.

"What's going on?" he asked, rubbing the side of his head.

"Nothing," I answered. It was the best answer I could come up with on short notice.

"Is that my hair in those tweezers?" He squinted at the hairs.

"I wanted a lock of your hair to put in a locket to wear around my neck," I said.

"Are you crazy?" He took the tweezers and frowned at them. "You don't get a lock of hair by jerking out a few hairs at a time! That hurt."

"I'm sorry. Okay, I'll tell the truth. You have six white hairs and I was trying to pull them out before you saw them and got upset," I explained.

"Oh, I already noticed them. It's no big deal," he said and handed the tweezers back to me. I looked at the hairs in the tweezers. None of them were white. I'd grabbed the wrong hairs—the six white ones were still there.

"I missed them. Can I try again?" I leaned forward.

"No! I'd rather have white hair than be bald!" He moved away from me. "Are you worried about me having white hair or about us getting older?"

"Older," I admitted. "I didn't know we were getting older until I noticed you had white hair. I thought we were still young."

"We have four teenage children. Wasn't that a clue?" he asked.

"Not really because when I look at them they are still my babies," I sighed.

"You know, I think you are prettier now than when I married you," he said. "You look younger every day."

"You're lying, but thanks for making the effort." I flopped back onto the bed. "I'm old. You're old. We're old."

"We are approaching middle age, that's all. We still have another forty or fifty years ahead of us," he said.

"Let's have another baby," I said, which seemed like a great idea to me.

"I don't want another baby, Cry. I'm glad the kids are growing up. I'll be glad when the boys are old enough to be partners on the farm. I'll be glad when they all get married and move out," he said.

"How can you be so mean?" I asked.

"I'm not being mean, I'm being realistic. Everyone gets older every day, every hour. I don't mind getting older. I'm tired. I'm looking forward to retiring and taking life easy. I'm looking forward to a time when there is just the two of us again. I'm not old but I'm too old to start another family," he said.

I wrapped my arms around myself. I felt as if I'd lost something. The truth was I did want more children. I wanted babies in the house again. I wanted cribs and diapers and middle of the night feeding and I wanted to be needed again.

"Maybe one of the boys will get married soon and you'll have grandchildren," Don suggested.

Telling a woman who is having a mid-life crisis that she could be a grandmother soon isn't the smartest thing Don has ever done.

Of course, I was convinced I would make a terrific grandmother and I was looking forward to it, but I didn't feel like I was ready to give up being a mother yet.

"Fine," I said, "I'll just get old and sit in my rocking chair and knit."

The next day I noticed the six white hairs were gone. I don't know whether he got rid of them for me or for himself.

* * *

People say marriage is a compromise but it isn't. There are hundreds of times when you can't compromise; one person has to give up, surrender and face total defeat. I wanted more children but Don didn't. You can't have half of a child or be parents half the time. It is all or nothing and this time it was nothing.

I felt sad in a way only other women could understand. I don't think it would matter if you had one child or twenty children. When you knew there weren't going to be any more there was still a sense of loss. My heart and my body longed for another child but my mate did not want any more children.

Sometimes men, even good men, don't understand women.

Sometimes, compromise means one partner has to lose. It

was a lonely time for me. Losing Holly had left a big hole in my heart and I couldn't find anything to fill it. I missed my friend.

Of all the mysteries in life, one of the greatest is friendship. I don't understand why we become friends with one person and not another or why some friendships last a lifetime and others die after a few months.

I used to think that a really good friend was a friend forever and that nothing could ever come between you. When friends would move away I would write to them, ignoring the fact that their letters would get fewer over time until at last we were only exchanging Christmas cards and finally not even that. I am always the last to let go of a friendship.

It has taken me a long time to learn that some friends are meant to be temporary, like an angel who just crosses your path and is gone. It is hard to let go of friendships without wondering if you did something wrong or being hurt because you were dropped from their lives.

Since I never had any brothers or sisters, my friends are especially important to me. They take the place of the family I never had.

I've never met two of my best friends. We've been pen pals for twenty years and exchanged thousands of cards and letters. Joanie lives in New Jersey and Denise lives in Alaska and we will probably never see each other face to face but I couldn't feel any closer to them if they lived next door. When I'm really happy, I write to them. When I'm really sad, I write to them. We often think of each other on the same days and our letters cross in the mail.

People don't write letters much anymore. They use e-mail or the phone and I guess it is good to hear someone's voice, but I like letters. I can save them and read them again, I recognize my friend's handwriting. I can tell if she is scribbling because she is upset or in a hurry or excited. I feel sorry for people who don't get letters from friends. It must be depressing to just get bills in the mail. Nothing brightens up my day like a card or letter from one of my friends.

Cards and letters, though, aren't the same as being with someone. Joanie might love the funny birthday card I sent her but I can't hear her laugh when she opens it. Denise might feel better when she receives the Get Well card from me but it would be better to show up at her door with a flower and bowl of chicken soup.

My life was changing and I wasn't ready to grow old gracefully. I didn't want my friends to die; I didn't want my husband to have white hair; I didn't want my children talking about leaving home. I didn't want to be alone. I finally had to admit my greatest fear was the fear of being alone and lonely.

Loneliness is something I have battled all my life. When I was a small child of four and five I was left alone for long periods of time. I was often left in the care of my uncles who would feed me dinner, tell me to go to bed and go to sleep. Then my uncles would spend the night partying with friends, leaving me alone in a small, dark house until the next day when they'd come home with hangovers from drinking all night.

As soon as I heard them drive away I would get out of bed and sit on the floor beside the front door, my hand on the door-knob. I was afraid to stay in the house, afraid to go out of the house, terrified of every shadow and sound until I'd fall asleep crumpled on the floor.

If I were lucky I'd wake up before my uncles came home and crawl back into my bed, pretending I'd been there all night. Sometimes I'd still be asleep on the floor and they'd have to push against the door to shove me aside so they could come in.

I began to have nightmares and to sleepwalk. One of my uncles put a big hook on the outside of the front door so they could lock me inside when they left because they were afraid I'd wander outside while I was sleepwalking and get lost or freeze to death.

The nightmares that started when I was four never stopped and never went away. After I'd grown up and moved away, the sleepwalking dropped to just once or twice a year but the nightmares continued.

Before we were married I warned Don that I didn't sleep well at night, that I had nightmares and sometimes even walked in my sleep. The poor man had no idea what was in store for him.

I still have nightmares almost every night. I don't go to bed until about two o'clock in the morning and I usually wake up by six. Sometimes the nightmares are so bad I wake up screaming. I'm surprised I haven't given Don a heart attack. There is nothing quite like having your wife curled up asleep next to you one minute and then having her let out a blood curdling scream the next minute.

I've tried everything under the sun, moon and stars to get rid of the nightmares. I've tried prayer, tried exercises, reading, listening to soft music, medication, counseling and sleeping in every possible position but the nightmares are ghosts from the dark and distant past that haunt me at night when I'm asleep.

I don't know what causes dreams. Some people say they don't dream at all (Don says he can't remember having a single dream in his entire life). Some people say they had a few nightmares when they were children that they outgrew. Doctors have told me dreams are chemical reactions in my brain and, for some reason they don't understand, my brain doesn't sleep when my body does. My brain thinks it is still awake and works at the same speed it does during the day. Ministers have told me I must have a problem in my spiritual life or my relationship with God. I don't think that is true. I think I have a better relationship with God now than at any time of my life. I don't think it is any of these things. I think I have nightmares because I was alone too much when I was a child.

I think I continue to have nightmares because even though I have God, and a husband, and four children, and friends, somewhere deep down in my heart I'm afraid I'll be alone again someday.

Chapter Fourteen

FADED PHOTOGRAPHS

If I could only keep one possession for my entire life I would keep the photographs of my family and friends. Everything else can be replaced. We might mourn the loss of special keepsakes or antiques but most of the things we have in our homes can be replaced. Once a photograph is lost, it is lost forever. That moment in time is gone. Children grow up, friends move away, seasons change: nothing is ever the same as that single moment again.

My family often teases me because I have taken hundreds of photographs of them. I have countless albums filled with these precious pictures. I tell them that someday, after they have all grown up and left home, these pictures will be all I have left and they are worth more than gold to me.

I am faithful to write the names and dates on the back of each photograph and sometimes I add a few words about the reason for the picture because it is easy to forget.

I have only three photographs of my ancestors that date back more than sixty years. One is of my grandparents standing in front of a tipi looking awkward and embarrassed. My grandfather, who was a very short man, wore cowboy boots to make him just an inch or so taller but he was still shorter than my grandmother was. In the photograph he was almost the same height as she was. If you study the photograph enough, you can see the marks on the ground in front of him where he scuffed up enough dirt to make a small mound of dirt for him to stand on so he would look taller in the photograph.

It is the only photograph I have of them but it tells me a lot about them. Grandfather seemed ashamed of being shorter than his wife, who was a year older than he was and tried to look bigger than he was. Grandmother's long cotton dress was badly wrinkled which could mean she either hated to iron clothes or that the photograph was unexpected because I think if she'd known about it ahead of time, she would have ironed her dress and combed her hair. They almost look afraid. They certainly don't look happy and they are not smiling. They are young in the picture but they already look old. Their eyes are dull and there is no trace of humor in them. Their life together must have been hard from the very beginning because the photograph was taken before they had any of their eleven children and before they'd lost six different farms and before two of their children died.

I look at the picture and wonder if they were ever happy or ever had any fun.

I have another photograph marked "Aunt Elizabeth and Family" that was dated 1885. I knew the story about Aunt Elizabeth and Uncle Robert and the terrible day they had when their family portrait was taken.

Elizabeth loved everything about Robert—well, almost everything. Robert's family tanned raw hides and she couldn't bear the terrible smell of rotting animal flesh.

Before paying a courting call on Elizabeth, Robert would scrub his skin until it was raw and splash on bay rum cologne. Elizabeth would still hold a perfumed handkerchief to her nose and swear the smell of death followed him like a cloud. She could not marry a man who earned his living skinning carcasses to make leather.

Robert's family was angry and insulted. Dealing in hides was honest work and somebody had to do it. Did this silly girl think leather grew on bushes? Robert's father and two brothers earned a good living dealing in hides and Robert was lucky to have a family business to go into. They thought Elizabeth was too proud and that Robert deserved a better wife who would appreciate him.

Elizabeth would not give in, Robert was in love so he left his family behind and married Elizabeth and moved to a small farm in the middle of the Kansas prairie.

Robert wasn't much of a farmer and they barely raised enough food to eat. Robert felt guilty for letting his wife suffer;

Elizabeth felt guilty for dragging her husband away from his family and a good paying job but they were both too proud to crawl back to his family to ask for help.

They had two daughters, Sarah and baby Emily. In the spring of 1885 whooping cough swept through the little settlement and hardly a family escaped the terrible cough. When Sarah and baby Emily got fevers and began the wracking coughing, it looked as if they wouldn't live much longer. Elizabeth blamed herself that her babies were dying. She felt if only she'd stayed in Missouri and let Robert work for his father none of this would have happened. It was her pride and vanity that had caused all of this suffering.

"My children are going to die and we don't even have a picture of them!" Elizabeth sobbed. "We'll forget what the poor little darlings looked like!"

The children were too sick for the long ride to town so Robert took the money they had saved for a plow, rode into town and brought a photographer back to the farm. Elizabeth, who was still proud, didn't want Robert's family to see their shabby cabin, so she hung a bedspread on the wall and covered a box with a shawl for the children to sit on. She wanted the photograph to look as if it had been taken in a fine studio instead of in front of a cabin on a barren farm. The sick children were then dressed in their best clothes for the one and only picture that would ever be taken of them.

The little girls were fussy and afraid of the camera. Elizabeth burst into tears every time she thought about the reason for the photograph. Robert's face was grim. He could send his parents a picture of his daughters, but they would never get to see them alive. There had never been a more miserable family getting a picture taken—and it showed.

In the end, Sarah and Emily did not die. They recovered from the whooping cough before the photographer even got the photographs back to Robert and Elizabeth. To Elizabeth's dismay, the bedspread hadn't disguised the log cabin. In addition, the shawl spread over the box had holes in it. They were poor and it showed. Elizabeth swallowed her pride and sent the picture to Robert's family and asked their forgiveness.

Robert's family wanted their granddaughters with them, not stranded out on a desolate homestead where another epidemic might really kill them. They made Robert an offer: he could come home and he would not have to work with the raw hides. He could work with the finished leather and make saddles. He wouldn't have the smell of death around him that Elizabeth had hated so much.

Robert and Elizabeth left the farm and took their daughters back to Missouri. Robert's family welcomed them home with a better job for Robert and a comfortable house for the family. The very people Elizabeth had scorned had rescued them and welcomed them home with open arms. Elizabeth was now a happy woman. Sarah and Emily grew up to be strong, healthy young women and had large families of their own.

No other photographs were ever found of the family. If they had others taken, they were lost or given to other relatives. The only one they left behind captured the very worst moment of their lives.

* * *

There is also a picture of two young women standing proudly beside a clothesline filled with freshly washed laundry. It is a picture of the Great Laundry War.

My aunts, Dottie and Jane, were only in their teens at the time the photograph was taken. They'd left the farm and moved to town where they hoped to either find husbands or jobs. They found husbands: they married brothers. They would have been very happy except they had to share a house and that house was next door to their new mother-in-law who was not happy about losing two sons at the same time to a couple of poor country girls.

Their new mother-in-law constantly criticized the two young brides, finding fault with everything they did and always made comments about how lazy they were.

The mother-in-law firmly believed in the old housewife's rhyme:

Wash on Monday, hang it on the line;
Iron on Tuesday, do it fine;
Mend on Wednesday, don't you whine;
Clean on Thursday, make it shine;
Shop on Friday, spend a dime;
Bake on Saturday, so we can dine;
Church on Sunday, act real fine.

The mother-in-law believed a woman washed clothes on Monday. It was the law. Any woman who didn't have her laundry hung out by 8:00 Monday morning had better have had a death in the family, or, at the very least, two broken arms. She had strict rules about how things should be done. Laundry was never washed on Sunday. Laundry hung out on Tuesday made her frown and shake her head at her bad luck having two such lazy daughters-in-law.

To make her point, the mother-in-law had the whitest, brightest laundry in the neighborhood and always had it on the line by eight o'clock every Monday morning.

Dottie and Jane were determined to win the respect of their mother-in-law and would get up early to have their laundry washed and on the clothesline by 7:30, beating their mother-in-law by thirty minutes. The next week, the mother-in-law had her laundry hung out by 7:00. The following Monday the girls hung their laundry out at 6:30 knowing what would probably happen next week—the mother-in-law would probably be doing her laundry in the middle of the night so she could hang it out as soon as the sun came up.

Dottie and Jane decided to declare War. They loved their new husbands and they had tried to be friendly with their new mother-in-law but if she wanted War, then they were just the girls who could give it to her!

For the next four weeks, no matter how early the mother-in-law crawled out of bed and washed her clothes, by the time she dragged the baskets of laundry outside she was greeted with a clothesline filled with bright, clean, laundry, Dottie and Jane relaxing, enjoying their morning coffee.

She decided she was too old to try to keep up with the young brides, especially when they were such hard workers and did their laundry before the sun even came up!

The mother-in-law bragged to everyone about how lucky her sons were to find such good wives and constantly praised her daughters-in-law for being such hard working girls.

Dottie and Jane and their husbands soon saved enough money to move into their own homes miles away from their mother-in-law.

Dottie and Jane had won the Laundry War by using their secret weapon. They weren't getting up before dawn like everyone thought. Before they went to bed on Sunday night they would grab some clean sheets and towels and clothes out of the closet and go outside in the dark to hang them on the clothesline. No matter how early the mother-in-law got up on Monday morning, she was greeted by clean laundry flapping in the breeze.

Most people would look at this photograph and just see a picture of two young girls standing beside a clothesline and wearing big smiles. They wouldn't know they were looking at the victorious, brave and very clever Generals who defeated their enemy in the Laundry War.

I knew the stories behind these family photographs. I've written them down for my children because, otherwise, they would only see a picture of a couple posing in front of a tipi, a picture of a man and wife and their two babies and a picture of two girls doing laundry. There is so much more to know about these people. They were afraid and shy, embarrassed, proud, strong, clever and funny.

The photographs we leave behind are important because someday our grandchildren or great-grandchildren will only know us through our faded old photographs.

* * *

When Don was invited by his cousins to a family reunion he didn't want to go. I'd never met this part of his family and thought it was a good idea for our children to meet his distant relatives.

We drove 500 miles to Texas. The trip wasn't fun. The weather was over 100 degrees, the car didn't have an air conditioner, the driver didn't want to take the trip in the first place and four hot, bored children were complaining in the back seat.

When we arrived at the reunion we discovered several things. Don's family speaks "Texan" with a heavy southern drawl and we couldn't understand half of what they were saying. The "cousins" I'd wanted the children to meet were in their seventies and didn't want to play games: everyone at the reunion was over seventy years old.

Don realized he not only didn't recognize anyone at the family reunion, he'd never heard of them. After talking to everyone there he came to the conclusion that all they had in common was the last name "Stafford" and he must have been invited by mistake. The invitation must have been meant for some other Stafford in our town.

"How could you let this happen?" I whispered to him. "How could you not know they weren't your relatives?"

"I've been out of touch with my family for thirty years," he whispered. "Besides, you were the one who wanted to come to this reunion so our kids could play with their cousins!" We both looked at the elderly people sitting in lawn chairs fanning their faces and sipping iced tea. Every one of them was a complete stranger to us.

"Don't feel bad," an old woman smiled at Don, "We have the same last name, we must be related . . . somehow."

"Well, I'm sure we are but I think we've made a mistake and I think we'll be leaving now. Do you know where we can get a room for the night?" Don asked.

The old woman laughed. "The nearest town is forty miles away but it doesn't have a hotel. It is getting late and the children look tired. You might as well spend the night with us, even if you aren't among family, you are among friends," she smiled.

That was our second big mistake.

The house was taken up with all the people who belonged there. Every bed and sofa was filled while the "younger" people in their sixties slept on mats on the floor.

Don and the boys decided to take their chances with wild animals and mosquitoes and sleep on blankets on the ground under a tree. Spring Storm and I lay down in our car, I was in the front seat and she was in the back.

"Mom, I'm starving," she pleaded. "Isn't there anything to eat?"

"I'm hungry too. Let's see what is left in our picnic basket." We hadn't eaten in hours and I was starved.

We found two cans of warm soda and a bag of candy. It was dark and I spilled some of the candy in the car seat. Spring Storm and I felt better after we'd eaten. She curled up like a pretzel in the back seat and I was twisted up like a corkscrew in the front seat.

"You know, dear, this is going to be a funny memory and someday you'll laugh about how your family went to the wrong reunion and you had to sleep in a car and live on candy and warm soda." I tried to cheer her up.

"I've learned one thing today," she yawned. "If I ever get married, I will marry an orphan so I will never have to go to a family reunion."

At six o'clock a lady pounded on the car window telling us to wake up. "Some of the family is leaving and we want to get pictures of all of us before they go," she said.

"But we aren't part of the family . . . " I reminded her.

"Well, we can't take that chance. Somebody might figure out how we're related later on and we want pictures," she said.

My right foot was tangled in the steering wheel and I was completely numb. I felt paralyzed from the nose down. My neck was so stiff I couldn't straighten my head.

"Every inch of my body hurts," Spring said on the verge of tears. "I want to go home, I want a hot bath, I want hot food. Mother, help me!"

"We'll be going home soon," I promised.

She peeked over the car seat and stared at me. "Mom! What happened to you? Your face is all spotty and weird looking!" she wailed.

I looked into the rear view mirror. I'd slept with my face on the candy I'd spilled on the car seat the night before and they'd melted on my face. The colored dye in the candy had left green, red and orange spots on my face. My face also had about twenty swollen mosquito bites. My hair was scrunched up into a big knot on the side of my head. It was all right, I'd be fine as soon as I could shower and wash my hair and change clothing.

We staggered out of the car and found Don and the boys. Snow Cloud had slept with his face on the zipper of the sleeping bag and it left a mark on his cheek that made him look like a Frankenstein monster stitched together by a mad scientist. Don needed a shave and all of us had slept in our clothing that was now wrinkled. My neck was so stiff I had to hold my head crooked to ease the pain.

We were pushed and shoved into a line of people while cameras clicked and snapped as dozens of photographs were taken. Photographs of the Stafford reunion would be hung on walls and put into albums and a hundred years from now other generations of Staffords would look at the photographs of all the clean, neat, nice looking elderly people. Then they would point at the family of six in the group and ask, "Who are those dirty people in the wrinkled clothes? What are those awful spots on that woman's face and why is her head crooked? Why didn't any of them comb their hair? Those horrible, disgusting people can't possibly be related to us!"

And they would be right. We weren't related to any of them, but we'll be included in their family albums forever.

Chapter Fifteen

MY NAME IS AARON

Everyday I take at least a fifteen-minute walk with each of my children. We've done if for years. In the beginning, when they were small, their little legs often got tired and I'd have to carry them home. Now any one of them could probably carry me home.

As soon as dinner is finished, only the food is put away. The dishes are left for later.

Spring Storm and I usually go for our walk first. We walk up to the pine grove and sit on a bench and talk about our day or about nothing. Sometimes we walk to the pond and skip rocks across the surface or throw breadcrumbs to the ducks. Spring has an inner happiness that lights up the world around her. She is as delicate and as graceful as a swan but never hesitates to explore caves, climb trees or catch lizards with her brothers.

On our way back to the house we walk past an old stone foundation. It is all that remains of a house built in 1910. Spring and I have planted a flower garden inside the foundation. The stone walls that once marked off rooms now separate iris, bachelor buttons, jonquils and daisies. The first crocus in the spring bloom along the path here. Two lilac bushes that were planted long ago still produce huge, heavy clusters of lavender lilacs.

Sometimes when we are digging in our garden we find marbles and pieces of toys and broken china that belonged to that long ago family. We leave them in our garden. We like to think that long ago family is still around someplace.

Snow Cloud and I go out next. He is the most adventurous of the children and likes heading for the stony brook in the hollow. We climb over fallen logs and sometimes he swings from grapevines yelling like a wild man. He likes to talk about the news and what's going on in the world and since he is always better informed than I am, I always return to the house knowing more than when I left. Snow Cloud knows all the plants and can find flowers so small I think only ants could know they exist. His gentle touch is a special gift and plants and animals flourish under his care.

Lost Deer and I go for our walk next. He can never leave the world the way he finds it. He always has to "fix" something on every walk. He moves a rock, pulls a weed, straightens a flower. He always leaves things better than he finds them and he always has a funny story to tell. It's hard to spend five minutes with him without sharing a good laugh. It's impossible to be sad or worried when Lost Deer is around: he's like a huge yellow sun, bursting with laughter and sheer joy. Every minute of every day is an exciting adventure to him.

Little Antelope and I go for our walk last. The sun has already set and the owls and whippoorwills are beginning their twilight talk. Little Antelope has always been the serious, quiet one, choosing books for his best friends. Since he learned to read at the age of four he has always asked for books for gifts and his room looks like a library. I especially treasure our walks because he is nearly grown. He'll be gone soon and our walks will be gone with him.

It has always been a good time to talk about problems, away from the rest of the family, away from the activity and noise in the house. It felt good to be alone with each child for awhile at the close of the day. Wind, rain and snow didn't stop us but did sometimes shorten our walks.

Some walks were so special we would always remember them. Most walks were just a pleasant break in the day. Some were painful beyond belief.

"Mom, I have to tell you something," Little Antelope said and sat down on the swing that hung from the huge old oak tree.

"I'm listening," I watched him as the swing swayed silently.

"I don't want to use my Indian name anymore. I only want to be called Aaron, not Little Antelope," he said without looking at me.

"All right." I was glad my voice remained even. "That is

why we gave all of you children both Indian and non-Indian names . . . so you could choose."

"I'm too old to be called Little Antelope. I'm almost a man. Most of our Indian friends stopped using their tribal names years ago," he said. "I want to start a new life."

"That's fine. It may take me awhile to get used to calling you Aaron but I will, if that is what you want," I agreed.

"Mom, it's not just me." He looked at the sky. "The others want to stop using their Indian names too. It makes life too complicated."

"They didn't say anything to me about it," I said. So, they'd been afraid to hurt me and they made Little Antelope, no, Aaron, do the dirty work.

"I'll tell them it is all right. I do understand. I've had trouble being 'Crying Wind' in a world of 'Jennifers' and 'Marys'," I said.

"It was wonderful being Indian when we were kids but now it is different. If I was a full blood I'd keep the traditions, but I'm as much White as Indian, and Mom, let's face it, it is easier to be White. I'm not ashamed of who I am, none of us are," he shook his head. "Please try to understand. I'm glad you taught us all the Indian ways but now I want to go other ways."

I nodded. I did understand but it hurt. "We'll call you Aaron and the other boys Shane and Trent," I said. "What does Spring Storm want to be called?"

"She is happy with her name for now but might want to

change it when she is older," Aaron said.

I lied. When the children were little I told them they had a choice: they could choose the Indian way of life or their father's way of life. I thought I meant it but I lied. I wanted them to choose the Indian way. I'd filled our home with Indian artifacts, Indian art, music and Indian food. I hadn't played fair. When they were little children they loved the Indian ways. There was so much freedom and fun but as they grew older they grew tired of the Indian ways and other paths looked more promising.

No, I wouldn't force them. I had my own little tribe for years. Now they no longer wanted to play cowboys and Indians. Buffalo jerky wasn't as good as pizza, stories under the stars couldn't compete with television and powwows were boring for them: most of the people were old. That was true. Some of the Indians at the powwows were close to a hundred years old. Their parents might have fought with Sitting Bull at the Little Big Horn and hunted buffalo.

They had a century of wisdom that would soon be lost forever but to a seventeen-year-old boy, they were just old people, old Indians who went to powwows and shuffled through the Gourd Dance because it was the only dance slow enough to dance to. They'd dance one time and then spend the rest of the evening with their shawls or blankets pulled around them and they'd watch the young people dance and whirl with feathers and drums and blood curdling yells. They'd remember when they were young and how they'd danced and how their grand-parents had danced the war dances but they'd been danced for real wars then. These were the last of the real Indians.

My children had chosen and I felt a little hurt they had not chosen my way. They were good Christians, good people, good children. How could I complain because they did not want to live in the past?

"Is that all that is on your mind?" I asked. How could there be anything more—wasn't this everything in the world?

"Maybe one more thing," his voice dropped so low I had to take a step closer to hear him. "A teacher at school told me I should go to college. He said I'd made straight 'As' through four years of high school and I could get into a good college. Mom, I hate farming. I'm tired of chopping wood, hauling hay and tak-ing care of animals," Aaron said softly. "I want to go to college."

No one in our family had ever gone to college. Don and I both came from people who farmed or were laborers. College was for rich people in cities, not for people like us.

Not for people like us? Why not for people like us? Just because we were poor and lived on a farm didn't mean that Aaron wasn't as smart as other people. Why shouldn't he get to follow his dreams? I would not stand in his way; I would not hold him back.

"You do what is best for you, do what will make you happy and your family will stand behind you and help in every way we can," I promised.

"The teacher said I might be able to get a scholarship but that would only pay for half of the expenses and college costs a lot, more money than we have." Aaron was discouraged, it echoed in his voice.

"Don't worry about money," I said. "You must never let money make your decisions for you." Aaron laughed. He knew as well as I did we'd had a disastrous year and there had been weeks when we'd lived on pancakes and nothing else. Aaron, my first little baby was now seventeen and wanting to go to college. I wanted him to be a little boy again but I couldn't turn back in time.

"Go ahead and do whatever you need to do to get enrolled in college. Talk to your teacher; ask him to help you with the paperwork. You will go to college," I promised.

We walked back to the house that already seemed empty. Aaron was walking beside me but his mind was in college far away. My first born would be leaving home and I tried not to let my tears go but with every step my heart whispered, "He's going away, he's leaving home, I'm losing my son, my first born, Little Antelope." I told Don what Aaron said.

"I thought he'd stay here and help on the farm. I was counting on him and the other boys. I thought with their help we could buy more acres and have more animals. He never said anything about not wanting to work the farm." Don felt betrayed. "I guess none of the kids will grow up to be cowboys or Indians . . . or farmers."

He smiled at me, trying to cheer me up but it didn't work. I shook my head, afraid I'd cry if I tried to speak.

"Remember how we spent hours talking about how we'd teach the kids about Indian ways and about farming and following in your footsteps or my footsteps? They didn't take after either one of us; maybe they'll all go to college and live in the city. I wonder what we did wrong?" He shook his head.

I had to give a little laugh, a sort of half-happy, half-sad laugh. I was acting as though Aaron was doing something terrible. All the poor boy wanted to do was go away to get a good education so he could have a better life and more opportunities than we'd had.

"We didn't do anything wrong." I found my voice again. "We taught them to think for themselves and to be strong. I just didn't know it would hurt so much when they grew up."

"I feel like a dinosaur," Don said.

"I know, so do I, but we have been lucky. We had our own adventures; now it is their turn to have theirs," I said.

"Does he know how expensive college is? There isn't any way he can go this year. If he stays home and works on the farm then, when I sell some of the herd next spring, I can give him some of that money and he can use it to go to college. Next year," Don said.

Aaron wouldn't want to work on the farm another year hoping to get the money for college. If there weren't enough calves born or if it were a bad year, there wouldn't be any money and he would have wasted that year. No, I'd have to find a way to help him. Don did not want Aaron to leave the farm for at least another year and wouldn't help him leave any sooner than that. Don was unhappy because his son didn't want to be a farmer; I was unhappy because my son didn't want to be an Indian. Aaron was unhappy because he knew he was hurting his parents.

None of the children would follow in our paths. They wouldn't go to powwows, my daughter wouldn't make ceremonial dresses of buckskin, and she wouldn't spend hours sewing beads onto soft leather moccasins. Long ago when they were small they went to powwows and danced under the full moon, they danced around the fire to the beat of the drums. They played in the tipi and then they grew up. The past was disappearing a piece at a time like leaves falling from a tree.

"I hate letting go." I put my arms around Don's familiar waist and cried against his chest. "I hate it!"

I walked back outside and wandered around the yard alone.

The tipi looked as sad as I felt. The wind had torn pieces of it into rags and now they floated in the wind like gray hairs on an old woman's head. The paintings of bears and deer were so faded I could hardly make them out.

I remembered when the tipi was new. The canvas was clean and white, the designs bold reds and blues. It had been a beautiful tipi. We had spent so many hours sitting in it while I told the children the legends of our ancestors. We slept on Navajo rugs, we ate buffalo meat and fry bread. We were Indians. From the opening in the tipi, I'd watched falling snow and dancing stars and sunsets; I'd watched my children play and grow. Seasons had come and gone. Now the tipi was old and ragged. My children walked past it without even seeing it. It had stood here so long it had become invisible to everyone but me. It wasn't strong and beautiful anymore, it was ragged and pathetic and old and tired.

I built a small campfire in front of it and sat inside of the tipi and watched the moon come up over the distant hills. I softly chanted a song older than time and when I was too sad to bear it any longer; I stepped outside and ran my hands over the painted deer. I walked around the outside of the tipi one last time; then I pulled a burning stick out of the fire and touched it to the canvas.

The flame crawled up to the top of the tipi. In a few minutes it was covered with flames. The fire hid the holes and the faded pictures and for a few seconds it looked brilliant and new. Then it collapsed into a heap of sparks that shot up as high as the moon and joined the stars.

I stood there until only a few embers were left of my once beautiful tipi. I wiped the tears from my cheeks and walked toward the house. Aaron stood in the shadow of the oak tree; I don't know how long he'd been standing there. He didn't speak; he just walked beside me.

There was nothing either of us could say.

Chapter Sixteen

THE SACRIFICE

Two weeks passed in a flurry of papers and letters and phone calls.

Aaron graduated from high school: yesterday he'd started kindergarten. The pain in my heart felt the same as it had felt the first day that he'd left for school. The two pains in my heart felt like seconds apart. But in reality they were years apart.

I knew I was running out of time and Aaron had to have the money for college now. I never dreamed college was so expensive. Aaron could get a student loan but I didn't want him to be in college with the burden of debt on his back.

We didn't have the money in the bank. The farm had lost money every year; crops failed, animals died, things broke down and wore out and had to be replaced. It was all we could do sometimes to keep food on the table.

Don was still upset that Aaron was not going to work the farm with him. He felt like college was a waste of time and that there was nothing wrong with working with your hands. He was not going to stop Aaron from going to college but he wasn't going to help him either.

I owned only one thing of value—my Indian ceremonial dress and the silver and turquoise jewelry that went with it. I'd spent nearly a year making the dress from four deerskins. It was as soft as a flower petal and the fringe was cut as narrow as pine needles. I got blisters on my hands from hours of cutting fringe. I'd sewn on sixteen pounds of colored glass beads in designs that told the stories of my family and my people. I'd worn the dress to powwows and ceremonies. It was as much a part of me as my name or my shadow. I picked up the dress and rubbed it against my face, smelling the rich leather. This wasn't a little cotton dress that was bought in a store, worn a few months and tossed away. The dress was a journal of my life.

I lay the dress down, picked up a silver and turquoise squash blossom necklace, some turquoise rings and a few bracelets; each one priceless with memories. I'd had most of this jewelry since I was a young girl, since before Don, since before the children. These were things an Indian woman kept all her life. She passed them on to her oldest daughter.

I placed my dress and jewelry in a bundle on a Navajo rug that a friend had woven for me and rolled it up. A woman named White Dove owned a trading post and had bought some beadwork from me in the past. I knew she would buy my dress and jewelry and I knew it was the only way I could get the money Aaron needed for college. White Dove knew how hard it was for me to sell my past but she knew it was for a good cause and she gave me a fair price.

I cried all the way home. I kept saying, "It is only a dress, I can make another one." But I knew it wasn't true. It was more than a dress and I would never make another one. I'd sold my past so that my son could have a future.

I gave the money to Aaron but didn't tell him where I got it. He wouldn't have taken it if he'd known I'd sold my dress and jewelry and Navajo rugs. I was proud of him. Nothing else was important.

Two weeks after he graduated from high school Aaron left for college. He was seventeen years old. He was happier than I'd ever seen him.

Chapter Seventeen

LIKE BIRDS LEAVING THE NEST

I held my son's high school diploma in my hands and read the name. "Shane Travis Lost Deer Stafford." Using his Indian name on his diploma was Shane's gift to me. I knew it would probably be the last time he would ever use the name "Lost Deer."

Two weeks later, at the age of seventeen, Shane entered the same college Aaron had entered exactly one year earlier. Two sons were now at college. Time was running through my fingers like water and while I was happy for my sons, I was sad for myself.

I never expected to be forty years old. That always seemed far away in the misty future. Then, one day, between cooking dinner and washing laundry, I turned forty.

Turning forty didn't seem like such a big deal until it happened to me. I wasn't old but I was no longer young. I was at a very strange in-between age.

It wasn't so long ago that most women died before they reached forty. Childbirth, disease and just plain exhaustion killed them off in their twenties and thirties.

Some days I felt as if I'd already lived a long time. Other days I felt as if I'd been a child just yesterday. If I was truly middle-aged, I had forty years ahead of me. I didn't want to waste them but I couldn't figure out what to do with them.

Don gave me a surprise for my birthday and took me horse riding. We galloped up hills and jumped over streams and trotted along forest paths for hours. It was glorious to feel the sun on my back and wind in my face, the sound of pounding hooves echoing the pounding of my heart. I felt young again.

"I'm dying," Don panted as he climbed off the horse and staggered to a fallen tree where he sat down. "I never did understand why people wanted to ride horses if they could drive a truck instead."

"I'm so lucky to have you," I said. "How many husbands would spend hours riding around on a horse just to make his wife happy?"

He smiled. The same smile I'd seen for so many years. "We'll grow old together," I promised, "and the children will come home and visit and bring our grandchildren."

"Do you think I could have you for myself for a while somewhere between all the kids leaving home and when they come back with the grandkids? I miss the time we had alone together when we were first married. I'd like to have it back before something happens," he said.

"We'll have at least fifty more years together because I know we'll both live to be at least a hundred years old." I took his hand. We walked for a while to give the horses a rest, although I think Don needed the rest, too.

"What would you like to do for your next birthday?" I asked. "If you could have anything in the world you wanted, what would you want?"

"I don't know. I guess more time with you, a little money, a better garden," he thought hard. "A new pair of boots."

"Don't you want more than that?" I asked, wanting to give him something wonderful to repay him for this special day.

"I don't need more than that," he said. "It doesn't take much to make me happy . . . although it would be nice if at least one of our children wanted to be a farmer."

Chapter Eighteen

INTO GOD'S HANDS

No matter how many times people warn us that life is short we never really believe them. We think we will have plenty of time to tell people we love them, to make peace with God and our families and to prepare our loved ones to face the future without us.

Don and I planned to grow old together. We talked about all the things we would do after the children left home. We planned trips that we would take together, we looked forward to big family holidays with our children and grandchildren. We thought we had all the time in the world.

We didn't.

Don died in a car accident while he was driving home from work. He was speeding and lost control of his truck and crashed into a bridge. He died instantly.

There was pain and emptiness beyond words. Our family was wounded. I had to deal not only with my grief, but also with an unexpected anger. I was angry with Don because he didn't have to die: he had caused the accident that took his life.

Don liked to drive fast. He was usually a good driver, especially if the children and I were with him. But when he was driving alone he liked to drive fast. He'd had several speeding tickets but he'd never had an accident.

Don was strong and healthy; he could have lived a long time and we could have grown old together. I felt cheated, the children felt cheated. He would not see his children graduate from college, or get married; he would never hold his grandchildren. The loss to all of us was almost unbearable.

The children and I clung to God and to each other. At first it seemed as if a hundred times a day I had to turn it all over to God but a few minutes later I would be asking "Why?"

Summer passed. The garden disappeared into a jungle of weeds: none of us had the heart to take care of it. It had been Don's garden and it hurt too much to even walk past it. He was everywhere. He was nowhere.

I began to blame myself for his death. I knew he liked to drive fast, I knew it was dangerous, I'd asked him to slow down a thousand times, I'd asked him to drive more carefully. I nagged. I worried. What if I'd tried harder? What if . . . what if . . . what if?

Snow Cloud's grief turned to rage against God and he refused to go to church. He needed time to heal and would have to do it in his own way. Little Antelope didn't return to college in the fall even though we all begged him to. He said he would take one year off to help on the farm and return to college the following year. Lost Deer and Spring Storm became quiet and withdrawn. It was as if our entire family was dying an inch at a time.

I was thrown from a horse and had to have emergency back surgery which left me in more pain than I'd ever experienced in my life. I was confined to bed for a month. It took another two months before I was completely healed and felt normal again.

I guess God had to put me flat on my back to get my attention.

When I came home from the hospital I still faced weeks in bed and I didn't want to spend hours and days in the bed Don and I had shared for so many years.

The children moved all of my things into what had been a small storage room. They put a narrow twin bed in the corner so I could look out the small window. The room seemed to be a symbol of my life. The room was small and dark and my life had suddenly become small and dark. Instead of sharing a big, wide bed with my husband, I was now sleeping in a narrow, single bed. I felt in my heart that this was how it was always going to be. I would spend the rest of my life alone in a single bed. I would not find love again; I would not marry again. I was alone. I would always be alone. I whispered the word "widow" for the first time and a numb coldness settled into my heart.

Because it had been a storage room there were no curtains on the windows, no pictures on the walls. It was dark, depressing and a perfect place to wallow in self-pity and feel sorry for myself.

Spring Storm came in and hung up a picture she'd torn out of a magazine. It had been an advertisement from some travel company urging people to go to Hawaii on their vacation. The picture showed a big yellow sun and blue ocean waves splashing onto the beautiful beach while tall palm trees swayed in the trade winds.

"I thought this would brighten up your room and give you something to look at. You can pretend you are walking on this beach." Spring Storm smiled as she hung it up.

In my mind I spent a lot of hours walking on that beach and wading in the ocean. It reminded me of the poster I'd hung in the hospital room for my friend Holly. She'd loved the ocean and dreamed of going to Hawaii but she died before she could make the trip. The world was such a beautiful place and I'd seen so little of it. I lay in my bed and thought about what it would be like to see the green hills of Ireland or the castles in Scotland. My daydreams took me to the streets of Paris and the fountains in Rome, to snowy mountain peaks and dusty deserts. No matter where my mind traveled my body stayed in the narrow bed.

If I hadn't seen much of the world my children had seen even less. The children had never seen the ocean and if I didn't do something about it, they never would. Their world had become small, their dreams had become small; soon, they would no longer have any dreams.

Aaron was chopping wood and repairing a barn on a farm he'd wanted to leave far behind. Shane was repairing cars for friends to make extra money. Spring was cooking and cleaning house like an old lady and Trinity was acting like a caged animal. I was afraid of what would happen to him.

I don't know when it happened but one morning when I woke up my back no longer hurt. Even more important, my heart no longer hurt. I could think about Don without being mad or sad. I finally accepted his death and I finally let go.

Our family didn't deserve special treatment in the world. Other people lost loved ones. Every day countless people died in accidents or from diseases—our family was no different. God didn't have favorite people that he protected from the bad things in life. We had grieved; We had mourned. It was time to pull ourselves together and start living again.

Lost Deer held my arm as I walked outside for the first time in over a month. The maple trees were scarlet. I'd never seen them so bright. In the pasture the oak trees were a rich golden tan. They were the color of Mark's hair. I remembered how Miss Neal had wasted seventy-four years waiting for her sweetheart to return. I wouldn't waste my life. I would get strong and healthy, our family would heal, grow and survive.

After that day our family life began to return to normal. We could laugh again and life seemed sweeter and more precious than it ever did.

Snow Cloud realized God hadn't reached down from the sky and stolen his father. Don had been driving too fast and had lost control of his truck. He'd made a mistake. It was a sad, terrible accident but it could have been worse. He could have hurt or killed other people. Snow Cloud found peace and his anger slowly faded.

Little Antelope began to make plans to return to college after Christmas.

I removed Don's chair from the head of the dinner table and replaced it with mine. I arranged the rest of the chairs so there was no longer an empty space at the table. We were a whole family. We were strong. We would survive.

Chapter Nineteen

A MERRY CHRISTMAS

In some ways it would be the most important Christmas we ever had. It would also be the hardest.

We were all determined to make it as happy as possible. We would decorate the house, invite friends to join us, have a big turkey dinner and exchange gifts. We would celebrate the birth of Jesus and the re-birth of our family.

A friend told us not to waste money on a Christmas tree and to come to his tree farm to cut down any tree we wanted. We drove to his farm several miles away and waded through knee deep snow looking for the perfect tree. The children argued about which tree was the prettiest, fattest, tallest and shaped the best until they finally agreed on one they all felt was perfect. They took turns chopping away at the trunk until the tree toppled over and we dragged it across the snowdrifts back to the car. We used a piece of rope to tie it to the rear bumper of the car and headed home.

As we drove the six miles home several people honked and waved and we waved back at them. Christmas was such a special time. People were so cheerful and friendly and seemed to have even more Christmas spirit than usual.

We arrived home, parked the car and climbed out. When we walked to the rear of the car to untie our beautiful tree we found nothing but a long, barren stick with a few broken branches sticking out of it. Our tree had come untied and we'd been dragging it behind the car for miles. The top part of the tree was missing altogether and there wasn't a single branch left on the rest that wasn't mangled. There wasn't a pine needle left in sight.

"That's why people were honking and waving at us!" Spring Storm said. "They weren't being friendly; they were trying to tell us that we were dragging a tree behind us!" We started to laugh and we laughed so hard we all collapsed into the snow. We laughed until our sides ached. We laughed until we cried and suddenly, the winter was warm again.

We drove back to the tree farm, picked another tree and cut it down. We tied it to the car and took it safely home and decorated it. It was a beautiful tree.

Outside in the yard, stuck in a snowdrift, stood what was left of the tree we'd dragged behind the car. The kids hung a few decorations on it which made it look even more pathetic but we kept it there because every time we saw it, it made us laugh.

It was a good Christmas.

Chapter Twenty

RISING UP FROM THE ASHES

We used a fireplace to heat our old farmhouse. In the early autumn it was an occasion to light the first fire of the season. The smoke would curl up out of the chimney and the smell of burning oak logs filled the air. The fireplace provided a cozy place in our living room.

A fireplace is not as romantic as it seems if it is your only source of heat. In the winter, a fire has to be kept going all day and all night. That means wood has to be cut and stacked in the yard. Someone has to carry the wood inside and there has to be kindling or wood shavings kept to start the fire. At night, bigger logs have to be stacked on the pile of hot coals to keep the fire burning all night.

The first person to get up in the morning has the job of cleaning out the ashes and starting up the fire to take the chill off the house before the others get up. It is a great deal of work and the fireplace really only heats the rooms in that part of the house. The bedrooms are so cold there is ice on the inside of the windows.

When I woke up on winter mornings, the first thing I would see was the picture still hanging on my wall. The big yellow sun, the beautiful ocean, the warm sand. I would try to keep that picture in my mind while I was hopping around the cold floor on my frozen feet trying to get dressed as quickly as possible so I could hurry to the living room and get a fire started in the fireplace so the chill would be off the room before the children woke up.

It was a bitter January morning, I'd built up a hot fire and had gone back to the kitchen to start breakfast.

The water pipes were frozen so I couldn't make coffee. I hoped the sun would come out soon and thaw out the pipes.

I began cooking eggs when I heard a roaring noise. Almost like a terrible windstorm. Although we lived in an area where tornadoes and thunderstorms often swept through in the springtime, this was January. It was too cold for such storms. I looked out of the kitchen window to see if someone had driven into the yard with a noisy truck but the yard was empty. Maybe one of the kids had turned on the radio and it wasn't working right.

I walked back into the living room and saw flames going up the wall around the fireplace! The chimney had caught on fire and now the wall and part of the ceiling was burning!

I ran down the hall where the children were still asleep and threw open the doors.

"Fire!" I screamed, "Get up! The living room is on fire!"

Little Antelope ran outside and grabbed the water hose but it was useless, the water pipes were frozen and we couldn't get a drop of water. He tried throwing shovels of snow at the house but it was a waste of time.

Lost Deer called the volunteer fire department and told them our house was on fire. They said they'd be right out but we knew it would take a while. Someone would have to phone all the volunteers, some of them were probably still in bed or out in their barns feeding their cows. They would have to drive into the little village and meet and then drive the fire truck to our farm that was six miles away. We would be lucky if they got here in half an hour, it would probably take longer.

The house was filling with smoke and I didn't see any way in the world we were going to save it. So far the fire was just in the living room, the bedrooms were on the far side of the house and were safe, for a while.

"We might lose the house," I told the children, "Go into your bedrooms, grab some pillowcases and throw in whatever you want to keep . . . just in case. Only take what is most important to you! Nothing is worth dying for! You have less than five minutes, then we'd better get out of the house and go stand in the barn. Hurry!"

It was easy for me to choose what I was going to save. My children first. Second, all of our picture albums. Everything else could be replaced, I didn't want to lose the photographs I had of the children and Don.

In less than five minutes the five of us stood in the barn door, shaking from the cold and from the fear. Behind us was a pile of pillowcases filled with photograph albums and trophies and a few clothes and a few toys.

Neighbors had seen the smoke and had driven over to help but without water, there was nothing anyone could do. A small group of people gathered around us.

One man I'd never seen before put his arms around me and hugged me, he had tears in his eyes. I don't know who he was but I'll never forget him.

The volunteer fire department arrived with their truck and a half dozen men arrived in cars. The house was too far gone, all anyone could do was stand there and watch as it collapsed in on itself and sparks and ashes and smoke flew up into the sky.

"We lost everything," Spring Storm whispered, mostly to herself.

"No, not everything. We are all alive, no one was hurt, each of us had time to save a few things that were most precious to us. All we really lost was some old clothes and some old furniture," I said. Of course, I didn't feel that way at all. I felt sick.

It's funny the things you think about. The half-cooked eggs on the stove. The wall in the hallway where I'd used a pencil to mark how tall the children had grown over the years and how I'd always moved the pencil line up a little to let them believe they were taller than they really were.

Cards and letters from friends, my paintings of horses and cowboys and Indians and mountains. My books. Gone.

I couldn't look at the children, I didn't want to know what they were feeling or thinking because it would have broken my heart. They were counting their own losses and I'm sure it was painful.

People came and went, several people offered to let us stay in their homes until we could decide what to do. Several people asked if we had fire insurance and I said no.

I don't know how long it took before the fire was out, finally, there just wasn't anything left to burn. The firemen poked around the still hot ashes trying to find anything they could save for us but there was nothing.

One of the firemen had been a friend of Don's. He said they'd talked about the chimney before and how it was so old and how some of the bricks were crumbling on the inside and that it wasn't safe anymore and he'd have to build a new chimney during the summer. He'd never mentioned it to me, I hadn't known there was a problem with the chimney. He probably didn't want to worry me because he thought he'd have a new one built before the cold weather came.

We didn't have any animals to worry about, we'd sold the last of them just before Christmas. There was no farm anymore, no animals, no house, just an old barn and some rocky ground and some trees.

We moved in with a neighbor while we tried to figure out what to do next.

We were broke and homeless.

A different neighbor made us an offer for our land, since it no longer had a house it wasn't worth much but since his farm joined ours, he was eager to increase his farm and he offered cash.

There was still a mortgage on the farm so by the time I paid off all of my debts I had very little left.

"What do you want to do?" I asked the children, "I have enough money for us to live two months. We can move to a town, rent an apartment and I can get a job . . . "

I knew what they were thinking. I'd been a mother and wife, I hadn't held down a paying job since I was a teenager. I didn't know how to use a computer, I didn't have any job skills. I couldn't imagine why anyone would want to hire me.

"We can all get jobs, if we all work and put our money together . . . " Little Antelope said.

"And do what? Live in a cramped little apartment in the city?" Snow Cloud said.

"What about college?" I asked Little Antelope and Lost Deer. They'd already taken off one semester to help on the farm. The longer they stayed out of school, the less likely it would be they'd ever return and graduate.

"What do you want to do, Mom?" Spring Storm asked.

I was tired. This year had been so hard. There had been so many struggles and disappointments and heartbreaks. Oh, there had been some victories and unforgettable moments, but right now at this minute, I was just tired. I didn't want to try anymore, I didn't want to be brave, I didn't want to have to start over, I didn't want to find a place to live and look for a job. All I really wanted to do was run away and hide.

"Mom?" Spring Storm asked again.

"To be honest . . . " I said, "All I really want to do is run away."

The kids laughed at my answer.

We were all huddled in a bedroom trying to plan our future. Our neighbors had been generous to let us stay in their home but we'd already been here several days and it felt strange being guests. We needed our own place, we needed a home.

"I have to walk," I said. I always did my best thinking while walking through the woods.

"Do you want to be alone or do you want us to come along?" Snow Cloud asked.

"Alone. I'll walk alone," I answered and walked out into the night.

Chapter Twenty-one

WHEN THE STARS DANCED

"Well, God, what am I supposed to do now?" I looked up into the star-filled skies.

"One of us has to do something pretty quick. I was sort of hoping it was your turn," I said.

It was freezing cold. I was wearing a borrowed coat that was too small and it wasn't keeping me warm and I was starting to shiver.

"God?" I called, "If you could just give me a hint, just push me in the direction you want me to go . . . "

My feet hit the ice and slid out from under me. I fell down and skidded across the ice, only stopping when I landed in a pile of crusty snow.

A long time ago, a friend told me that you never pray for rain unless you are carrying an umbrella. In other words, don't ask God for something unless you really want it. I'd asked him to give me a push in the direction he wanted me to go and now I was sitting in ice and snow in the middle of nowhere in the middle of the night.

And I was mad.

I hated ice and snow! I was sick of being cold six months a year. I was tired of never being warm enough. I was mad because our house had been so cold the morning I built the fire to warm it. I was mad that we didn't have a house that had a nice furnace and gas or electric heat. I was mad we heated our house with a fire pit like cave men. I was mad the water pipes had been frozen and we didn't have water to battle the fire. I was mad my husband was dead, mad my children were suffering, mad because I didn't know what to do next and mad about a hundred different things. But right now, at this minute, the thing that made me the maddest was this miserable ice and snow!

I kicked at the chunks of ice, I made snowballs and threw them at trees, I stomped my feet and left tracks all over the snowy meadow.

Finally, when I was through having a temper tantrum I lay down on the trampled snow and stared at the sky.

"I must look like an idiot."

The stars were still just as big and brilliant and bright. My tantrum had not made them move an inch or sparkle less. The stars were exactly the same as they had always been.

These stars were the same stars the children used to watch on hot summer nights and when they appeared to twinkle, the children thought they were dancing because I'd told them the universe was so happy when they were born that the stars danced in the sky.

I couldn't quite put my finger on it yet but I knew there was something stirring inside my heart. I was quiet so I wouldn't scare it away, like a deer making its way out of the woods, the idea was timid and could disappear in a flash.

"The same stars," I whispered. That was it. The same stars that used to shine down on me when I rode my horse through the night. The same stars that used to shine down on me when Don and I walked in the moonlight. The same stars that other people in the world looked at. Right at this very second other women, with even greater troubles than mine, were looking up at the stars and searching for answers.

Someone could be standing on a beach in Hawaii looking at the stars.

I could be standing on a beach in Hawaii looking at the stars.

No. I couldn't do that. My brain must be frozen. Just for a second I thought I could just run off to an island . . .

The kids had never seen the ocean.

What if . . . I didn't finish the thought. I was up and running back to the house.

"Thank you, God! Thank you, God!" I panted as I ran across the ice and snow.

I burst into the bedroom where all four kids were still sitting on the bed watching television.

I took off the coat and laid it on a chair.

"I fell down," I said.

"Are you hurt?" Spring Storm asked.

"No, I'm fine. I fell down on the ice and I was thinking about how much I hate ice and snow and being cold all the time. What if we never had to be cold again? What if we could just pick bananas and coconuts and lay on the beach? What if we went to Hawaii?" I asked in little short puffs of breath because I was still panting from running to the house.

"Are you talking about a vacation?" Little Antelope asked, "We don't have money for a vacation."

"No, not a vacation. Hawaii is just another state, it isn't a foreign country. We are just moving to a different state. Instead of moving to Kansas or Colorado, we'll just move to Hawaii. We'll live on an island and you'll see the ocean!" This was starting to sound like a good idea to me.

"Are you serious about running off and living on an island?" Snow Cloud asked.

"What do we have to lose? We don't have a home, we only have a little money but we have enough to get us to Hawaii. I have to get a job to support us no matter where we live. There are palm trees and whales and volcanoes and sandy beaches, warm, sandy beaches, and the same stars that are shining outside right now, are the same stars that shine on Hawaii." I was so excited I was almost jumping up and down.

"Could I go to college there?" Little Antelope's eyes were getting their twinkle back.

"Sure," I said, "Why not?"

"How soon would we go there?" Spring Storm asked.

"Tomorrow. We could leave tomorrow. Every day we stay here we have less money. If we leave tomorrow I will have enough money for our plane tickets and enough money to live on for one month. It's up to you, but think about it, this could be the greatest adventure we've ever had." No one spoke. "Being afraid is the most dangerous thing we can do."

"I want to see the ocean!" Snow Cloud said.

The very next night at midnight our friends drove us to the airport and waved goodbye as my four children and I climbed onto the airplane.

I don't know how the kids felt but I was shaking. The two things I feared the most in the world were water and flying in an airplane. Now I was going to be flying over an ocean. If there were a record of how many prayers could be said in one hour, I would have won a prize.

When the airplane landed on the Big Island of Hawaii we were overcome with joy. It was the most beautiful place I'd ever seen in my life. The airport was less than a fourth of a mile from the beach and it didn't take long until we were all running along the sand. I was even brave enough to wade in the warm, turquoise-colored waves, I wasn't afraid of water any more.

This beach could have been the same one in the picture that had hung beside my bed. There was a bright yellow sun and palm trees. The children were laughing and playing with the same carefree happiness they'd had when they were little.

It was a new life for them. For all of us.

Chapter Twenty-two

WE'RE STILL INDIANS

We were on an island in the middle of the Pacific Ocean. We were on the most remote island in the world, we were thousands of miles from the nearest continent. When I looked at a map, our island was barely a speck in the ocean. When I'd said we were going to "get away from it all," we'd gone as far away as possible without leaving the planet.

When most people think of Hawaii, they picture the island of Oahu and the city of Honolulu that is filled with tall buildings and shops and crowds of tourists. We were on an island hundreds of miles south of Oahu. We were on the Big Island.

The Big Island has a few small towns along the coastline but most of the island is uninhabited with thousands of acres of rain forests, waterfalls, palm trees and volcanoes.

There are five volcanoes on the island. The Kilauea Volcano is the most active volcano in the world and has been erupting continuously for the past sixteen years. The lava flows down the side of the tall volcano and plunges into the ocean causing a huge cloud of steam. The beaches have seven different colors of sand from white to green to black. The island has twenty-one different climates, from barren desert with cactus to snow on the highest volcano. There is no place like the Big Island in the entire world.

We were facing a completely new culture, ninety percent of the population was Native Hawaiian, Polynesian or Asian. For the first two weeks I don't think we understood anything anyone said to us and they didn't understand anything we said. Most people spoke a combination of Hawaiian, Pidgin English and Japanese. We soon learned that shoes were never worn into a house, shoes were always taken off and left outside of the front door. To wear shoes into someone's house was a terrible insult, it showed a lack of respect for their home and their family because you brought in dirt and trouble and bad luck from the outside world.

We were also much taller than most people, especially my sons who are very tall and were almost a foot taller than most of the people on the island.

We were very different. We were outsiders.

That's when I first learned about "Aloha." Aloha is the Hawaiian word for the spirit of love and friendship. It means everyone is welcomed with open arms and that everyone is "family."

I rented the first apartment I looked at. It was unfurnished and I bought each of us a pillow and a blanket. The man who owned the apartment was kind enough to loan the children a television. Our only furniture was a cardboard box to set the television on. We slept on the floor, we ate cereal three times a day, the children enrolled in school and I started looking for a job.

I applied for twenty-three jobs the first week and was hired for three of them. I was working eighteen hours a day scrubbing floors and doing housework, selling coconuts to tourists and working in a small café. I lived on one meal a day and lost twenty pounds. I was exhausted. Some nights when I got home from work I actually crawled up the stairs on my hands and knees, too tired to stand, too tired to walk. Some nights I fell asleep on the stairs. Sometimes I curled up into a knot on the bathroom floor, crying and shaking like a shell-shocked soldier.

I didn't know it at the time but I was suffering from something very similar to post traumatic stress syndrome. I may not have been in a war but I'd been through one trauma after another without any time to recover between them. Now I was working eighteen hours a day to support the five of us. On the outside I was calm and cheerful and brave and strong, but on the inside I was fighting panic attacks and depression. I didn't want the children to know that most weeks we were lucky to have even a handful of change left over. I was afraid if I lost even one of my jobs that we would be hungry and homeless in Paradise. I couldn't let my children down! I could not fail!

It wasn't exactly the romantic carefree life I'd pictured. I didn't spend a lot of time sitting on the beach, but we were in Hawaii and if we didn't give up, things would work out.

The children were making new friends and their friends were Hawaiian and had names like "Little Shark," "Dark Ocean Wave," and "Beautiful Flower Beside the Waterfall." Once again they were comfortable with their Indian names and began using them again with new pride.

Our apartment was only a few minutes walk from the beach and all of us would make several short visits a day to the beach. Every time I saw the ocean, it was like the first time. The color of the sea might change, the size of the waves might change, but the power, the mystery, the call of the ocean never changed. I was drawn to the ocean in a way I can't explain.

One evening while I stood on the beach watching the tide come in I thought about how much life was like the tide. People come and go through your life, good things and bad things come and go, like the tide. It is the natural way of things, nothing lasts forever, it is up to us to make the most of what we have and enjoy every minute.

I was living in one of the most beautiful places in the world. In my wildest dreams I never thought I'd end up on an island in the middle of the Pacific Ocean. The ocean was in front of me, there was an erupting volcano in back of me. I could see the red glow from the lava that bubbled and boiled inside of the crater.

It would spill out and flow harmlessly into the ocean on the other side of the island.

We'd made it this far but I was spending most of my time on my hands and knees scrubbing floors or working at one of my other jobs. I was gone most of the time, when I was home with the children I was so tired all I wanted to do was sleep. But we still took our nightly walks and I wouldn't have missed them for the world.

I walked barefoot in the sand, the ocean waves sneaking up and tickling my toes. The sun was down, the moon would soon climb up from behind the palm trees.

It was beautiful. I missed Don. I missed my friends. I missed the life I used to have.

"Don't look back," I told myself, "Don't look back." Looking back and having regrets is the biggest waste of time in the world.

"Well, God, you got us this far, you brought us thousands of miles to this beautiful island. Now what? I don't think you brought me here to scrub floors. What kind of job can I find that will pay enough so I can quit my other two jobs?" I asked.

The idea of one job supporting the five of us seemed impossible and I wanted the children to just attend school and not work. Their best chance for scholarships was to keep good grades. Little Antelope and Lost Deer were both back in college and I wanted them to stay there until they graduated.

We didn't have a car and couldn't afford to buy one, we

would have to walk everywhere for the next few months. I'd rented an apartment in a hurry to get us settled some place as soon as possible. I didn't know where the schools were or where the university was, I hadn't even thought to ask anyone. When I discovered our apartment was just two blocks from the university in one direction and two blocks from the high school in the opposite direction I knew I hadn't found this apartment by accident. There wasn't another apartment building in town that was as close to the schools as this one. It only took the kids minutes to get back and forth to their classes. It was as if God had reserved a place for us.

Strangers often left fruit on our doorstep, it wasn't unusual to open the door and find piles of bananas or pineapples or other fruit we'd never seen or tasted before. Everyone was so kind and helpful to us that we were often overcome by their eagerness to make us feel welcome.

I loved this strange and beautiful island but I knew I could not keep struggling just to survive from one week to the next.

One of my favorite verses in the Bible is, "Be still, and know that I am God." To me, that says everything that needs to be said. He is God, He is in charge, He knows what is going on in my life. All I have to do is be still. Be quiet. Don't move. Don't speak. Just wait and listen.

I sat on the beach and watched a sailboat head out into the open seas. I thought about that ship and how it had to set its sail either with the wind or against the wind, but it had to sail and not just drift. If it was allowed to drift it would be blown into the rocks and it would sink. If the anchor was dropped it might be safe from crashing on the rocks but it would never go anywhere.

I had fallen in love with the ocean and the ships that came and went. Sometimes a big sailing ship would come into port, a ship with tall masts and big canvas sails and rope ladders up to the crow's nest and they would make my heart leap inside of me. Before long I knew the names of all the ships and boats, I could recognize them from a distance like old friends.

"Someday," I thought to myself, "when the kids are grown and I'm alone, I'll sit on the beach and paint pictures of ships on the stormy seas."

I sighed. I used to paint a lot but that was a long time ago, I hadn't painted anything in years. There was so much work to do on the farm that there never seemed to be time to paint pictures.

I took a stick and drew in the sand. I drew a ship and it felt good. If I could paint pictures and sell them . . . I tried to figure out how many paintings I would have to sell each month to support the family. I could start writing again, I hadn't written any stories in a long time, I'd lost the heart for it. Maybe I still had stories to tell, maybe I still had pictures to paint. I might just be able to do it.

I was like that little sailboat. I could just lie at anchor and be safe but never go anywhere. I could just drift and end up another shipwreck, or I could choose my own fate and set my sail and head straight into the storm.

A few days later I was back on the beach painting a picture of an old sailing ship being tossed by waves on a stormy sea.

It wasn't long before several people were standing around watching me paint.

"How much do you want for it?" a man asked.

I was trying to get up the courage to ask a hundred dollars when Lost Deer joined me.

"She usually gets two thousand for a painting this size," he said.

I turned and stared at my son. The most I'd ever received for a painting was a few hundred dollars and that had been a long time ago.

I was getting ready to apologize for my son's joke when the man reached into his wallet and fanned through the bills.

"I have one thousand eight hundred dollars I'll give you right now," he said.

I couldn't even find my voice.

"Well, since it isn't framed, I guess we could let you have it for that. If it was framed you'd have to pay much more," Lost Deer reached out his hand for the money.

I'd never known anyone who carried that much money on them before. Any day I had twenty dollars with me I felt pretty rich.

Lost Deer carried the painting to the man's car and he drove away. We jumped up and down and spun around until people must have thought we were crazy.

The next day I quit all three of my jobs and stocked up on art supplies. I began painting old ships on everything from huge canvas to coconuts and rocks. I was doing something I loved and enjoyed and was making more money than I'd been making when I had three jobs.

I bought furniture and we were once again sitting on chairs and sleeping on beds and eating real food. We all breathed a big sigh of relief. A shop near the beach that catered to tourists began buying my smaller paintings, an art gallery near the volcano bought some of my larger paintings and whenever I painted on the beach, tourists would usually wander past and buy a painting or two. No one ever walked down the beach and offered me a large amount of money for a painting again, that had happened only once on the day I needed it the most. I guess God thought I needed a little encouragement.

I started writing again which was hard because I was writing about things close to my heart but the more I told my story, the less it hurt. By summer we were able to move into a house with a yard that had banana trees growing in it. We felt like we had a real home again.

The children and I still take our walks most evenings. We walk along the beach and wade in the surf and pick up shells.

In May, Little Antelope and Lost Deer will graduate from

the college. Spring Storm and Snow Cloud will both start college in the fall.

This isn't the life I planned when I was a young girl running along the dusty trails on the reservation. It isn't the life I planned when I married Don. It's the life God gave me, and that's good enough.

"What are you thinking about, Mom?" Little Antelope asked as the sun dropped lower in the sky and made the ocean look like melted gold.

"I was wondering how an Indian ends up on an island," I laughed, "It feels strange to be the only Indian here."

"You aren't the only Indian here, Mom, you brought your tribe with you," he said.

My children walked ahead of me, looking for driftwood. I'm proud of them, their father would have been proud of them too.

Life doesn't have to be perfect to be good.

Snow Cloud came to my side and handed me a seashell. "Do you still remember the Kickapoo War Cry?" he asked.

A moment later the five of us were running at break neck speed along the edge of the pounding surf, screaming Indian war cries at the top of our lungs.

Crying Wind and her tribe had arrived, the sea and the volcano were ours! We are warriors, we leap on you from the mountains, we fall on you from the sky! We are warriors and this is our home!

We are still Indians.

* * *

And Now . . .

Little Antelope graduated from university with a Masters degree in Business Administration. He lives in Seattle, Washington.

Lost Deer graduated from college with a Bachelors degree. He lives in Hawaii.

Snow Cloud graduated from college, served in the Navy and now has a small ranch in Texas.

Spring Storm graduated from university with a Masters degree in Anthropology. She lives in Hawaii.

Crying Wind still lives in Hawaii. She spends her time painting pictures of ships, walking on the beach and writing novels.

When the Stars Danced is her latest book.

Do you know the Creator's Son?

After reading *When the Stars Danced*, do you feel you know the Creator? Is He speaking to you? Would you like to respond to what you have just read?

Here are five things you need to know to believe in Jesus as your Savior:

You need to—

REPENT—Be sorry for the wrong things you have done—sorry enough to quit doing them. "God did not remember these times when people did not know better. But now He tells all men everywhere to be sorry for their sins and to turn from them" Acts 17:30.

CONFESS—Tell God you have sinned. "If you say with your mouth that Jesus is Lord, and believe in your heart that God raised Him from the dead, you will be saved from the punishment of sin" Romans 10:9.

BELIEVE—Jesus died for you. "Put your trust in the Lord Jesus Christ and you . . . will be saved from the punishment of sin" Acts 16:31

ASK—God to forgive you. "If we tell Him our sins, He is faithful and we can depend on Him to forgive us our sins. He will make our lives clean from all sin" 1 John 1:9.

RECEIVE—Jesus as your Savior. "He gave the right and the power to become children of God, to those who receive Him . . . to those who put their trust in His Name" John 1:12.

If you want to ask Jesus Christ into your life, pray the following prayer or pray in your own words what is printed below:

Dear Jesus, I realize I am a sinner. I long for peace in my heart. I believe you are the Holy Son of God, that you came down and died on the cross for my sins. Thank you for doing this for me. I am sorry for my sins. Please forgive me. With your help, I will turn my back on them. By faith, I receive you into my life as my personal Savior and Lord. From now on, I want to please You. In Your name, Amen.

If you have followed these steps and asked Christ to take control of your life, get a copy of God's Word, the Bible, and begin reading it. Also start talking to God in prayer. Go to church regularly. Choose a church where God's message of salvation is taught.

If you have prayed the above prayer, the publishers of *When the Stars Danced* would like to hear from you. Please write your name on the coupon on the following page, or if you don't want to cut up this book just write on another sheet of paper and mail it to:

In Canada:
Indian Life Books
P.O. Box 3765, RPO Redwood Centre
Winnipeg MB R2W 3R6

In the U.S.:
Indian Life Books
P.O. Box 32
Pembina, ND 58271

I prayed the prayer suggested in *When the Stars Danced* and now I would like more information on how to live as a Christian. Please write to me and tell me the name of someone who can give me personal help.

NAME _____

ADDRESS _____

TOWN/CITY _____

STATE/PROVINCE _____

ZIP/POSTAL _____

MORE HELPFUL READING

From the publishers of *When the Stars Danced:*

The Council Speaks

Here is a book which answers questions you may have had but were afraid to ask or didn't know whom to ask. You'll find questions dealing with pain, family life, culture, Christianity and the church. A council has answered these questions with honesty, insight and wisdom—all from a Native North American perspective. And all based on the Bible. This a book that just might change your life!

The Conquering Indian

An amazing collection of 70 stories showing that Jesus Christ can heal the deepest hurt of Native people. This book tells the stories of how these people, young and old, reached out to Jesus and how He answered their pleas and helped them to have victory over the problems they faced. You, too, can face up to your problems and conquer them. This book can be used to guide you to the One who can help you win that victory.

The Grieving Indian

Every Native person needs to read this book for the help and hope it offers. With over 75,000 books in print, find out why it has attracted so much attention.

Read one man's story of pain and hopelessness. Learn how his wife took a desperate step to turn his life around. This is a powerful book of hope and healing.

Indian Life

This newspaper is the most widely read Native publication in North America. In its pages you will find positive news of Indian people and events, first-person stories, photo features, family life articles and much more. Published six times a year. Write for a free sample copy. Find out why almost 100,000 people read this paper.

Does the Owl Still Call Your Name?

What grips and holds you captive? Is it alcohol, drugs, gambling, pornography, sexual addiction, solvent abuse, or thoughts of suicide?

Here is a book that goes beneath the surface of behavior and reveals the causes for addictive and abusive behavior and its results.

Not only are causes discussed. Cures are presented along with information on where help can be found.

Maybe you are gripped by one of the eight problems dealt with in *Does the Owl Still Call Your Name?* Perhaps you desire to help someone who is in the midst of a fierce battle. You will find helpful information and guidance about how to shine light to those in darkness and despair.

Are you a first time reader of Crying Wind's books?

We hope you enjoyed When the Stars Danced. Crying Wind also wrote her first book entitled Crying Wind as well as a second book My Searching Heart. Both of these were best-sellers and have been translated into a number of languages.

Sequoyah Editions is pleased to present these two best-selling titles in a new combined volume. Once again you can thrill to saga of Crying Wind as she writes frankly about past hurts and fears that would resurface later as she tried to begin a new life in Christ.

Stumbling upon Christ in her teen years, she found acceptance and encouragement through the patient, lovingkindness of a Christian couple. They encouraged her to move into life with Christ and into her gifting of poetic expression to share how past pain could not, in the end, halt her walk with Jesus. The results are her artwork and three books!

You can enjoy these books as thousands of others have! Available from Sequoyah Editions, an imprint of Indian Life Books.

Visit Crying Wind's website at www.cryingwind.com